THE WINDSURFING
FUNBOARD
HANDBOOK

THE
WINDSURFING
FUNBOARD
HANDBOOK
CLIVE BODEN AND ANGUS CHATER

BARRON'S

Woodbury, N.Y. Toronto London Sydney

A QED BOOK

First U.S. Edition 1984 by Barron's Educational Series, Inc.
Barron's Educational Series, Inc. has exclusive publication rights
in the English language in the U.S.A., its territories, and possessions.

All inquiries should be addressed to:
Barron's Educational Series, Inc.
113 Crossways Park Drive
Woodbury, New York 11797
International Standard Book No. 0-8120-5582-9
4567 987654321

This book was designed and produced by
QED Publishing Limited
32 Kingly Court
London W1

Designer Edward Kinsey
Editor Stephen Paul

Illustrators Susan Kinsey, Chris Forsey,
Gay Gallsworthy

Filmset by Text, Orpington, London
Origination by Hong Kong Graphic Arts Ltd
Hong Kong
Printed by Leefung Asco Printers Ltd
Hong Kong

Clive Boden and Angus Chater extend their special thanks to

Mary Saffian

windsurfing hawaii

Barry Spanier   Geoffrey Bourne

Rick Naish
Naish

Monty Spindler

Neil Pryde Sails

Windsurfers World, Hammersmith, London
Canon UK
Darrell Wong, Hawaii

CONTENTS

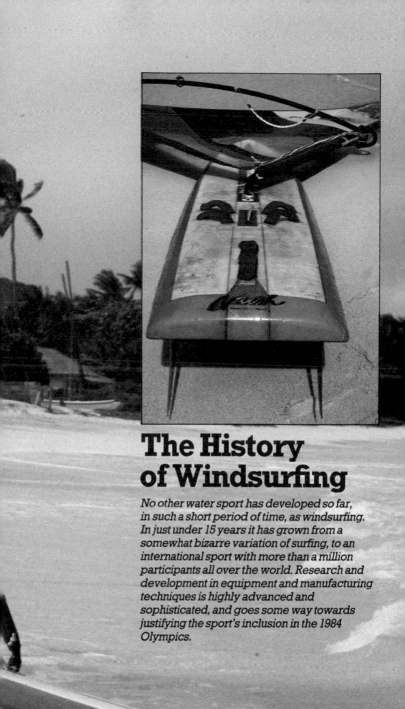

The History of Windsurfing

No other water sport has developed so far, in such a short period of time, as windsurfing. In just under 15 years it has grown from a somewhat bizarre variation of surfing, to an international sport with more than a million participants all over the world. Research and development in equipment and manufacturing techniques is highly advanced and sophisticated, and goes some way towards justifying the sport's inclusion in the 1984 Olympics.

The Beginning

The first account of a sailboard system can be traced back to August 1965, when a Pennsylvanian inventor called S. Newman Darby published his unpatented design in *Popular Science*, describing a 'New water sport for high speed water fun!' Darby's unusual craft had a square rig which was steered by pivoting the mast in its socket. Rather primitive and uncommercial in design, only a few were sold at the time. The durable Darby still sails his square rigger, and he was seen at Kailua Bay, Hawaii, demonstrating his unique craft to the world's superstars awaiting the start of the 1983 Pan Am World Cup.

Jim Drake Four years later the amiable American inventor Jim Drake – an aeronautical engineer who worked on the B70 bomber and the Cruise missile – presented his own paper to the first American Institute for Aeronautics and Astronautics Technical Symposium on Sailboat Design in Los Angeles. However, Jim Drake reports that the idea for a 'free-sail' system (steering by varying the sail position by means of a universal joint connecting mast to board) was discovered by a fellow scientist Fred Payne and himself as far back as 1961. Since then, hardly a boat show goes by without someone claiming to have invented the sailboard.

By 1967 Jim Drake was working on two free-sail systems – one with a universal joint on the mast foot, and another where the mast was fixed to the daggerboard, so that as the mast tilted forward the daggerboard rotated back. Both systems allowed the sail to swivel through 360° Working with him at the time was an enthusiastic Southern Californian called Hoyle Schweitzer. Eager to test their designs, Schweitzer ordered a board to be shaped to their specifications. Drake had still not finally decided how to attach the sail or control the board, but he eventually opted for a fully articulated universal joint on the mast foot and a double-sided wishbone boom arrangement. The test was a failure – mainly due to the absence of a rear skeg or a rope to pull up the mast. However, these problems were soon resolved and Drake and Schweitzer initiated a patent process to cover their invention in 1968. After finalizing the design of the appropriately named Windsurfer, Schweitzer went to work, producing a small number of Baja Boards made from plastic foam covered With fiberglass. Drake later sold his half of the patent to Schweitzer for a reputed $36,000 – a move he most certainly now regrets, not least in financial terms. He still takes a great interest in the sport he helped

Malte Simmer (left) performing what was, at the time (early 1980), considered a radical jump in Hawaii. He is sailing an early, first generation, square-tailed, custom wave jumping board.

develop, but no longer has any commercial interest in it.

Schweitzer and the patent Schweitzer took out the patent in as many countries as he could afford with his limited funds. He thought Germany, Australia, Japan, Canada and the UK would be the most likely countries in which the sport would succeed. Unfortunately he misjudged the interest in France, where the new sport took off and spread like wildfire. France and Germany are now the two largest markets in the world.

Production in the early days was extremely limited, and consequently the sport was very slow to develop in the US, and remained virtually unknown in Europe until the Dutch textile company Ten Cate started importing Windsurfers in 1970. By 1973 the US could no longer meet the demand and Schweitzer granted a license for Ten Cate to set up production in Holland. They are now probably the largest manufacturers of sailboards in the world. Not surprisingly, other European manufacturers were keen to exploit the increasing popularity of the sport, although many baulked at the 7½ % royalty per board Schweitzer charged for the license. Their main complaint concerned the ability of pirate manufacturers and manufacturers in countries not covered by the patent to undercut their board prices. Others tried to bypass the licensing laws by selling boards and rigs separately, while an even more elaborate scheme involved surf shops in Germany selling boards which the customer then 'collected' from shops in Austria. Schweitzer always maintained that his patent arrangements ensured that customers obtained high quality boards for their money – this was almost certainly a reflection on the poor quality boards France (which was outside the patent) initially produced. The result of these disputes was a series of lengthy legal battles between Schweitzer and the rogue manufacturers. These were ultimately resolved when Mistral, the largest Swiss manufacturer, lost their case in Munich in 1980, when German law upheld the patent. When the company was finally granted a license in 1981, they had to pay vast royalties. For a while, the situation in Europe became more relaxed, with more manufacturers accepting the royalty terms, but in the US, the process seemed to be starting all over again.

Peter Chilvers The patent dispute has consistently dominated the history of windsurfing, and judging by the events of January, 1984, it will continue to do so for some time.

In 1958, a young lad called Peter Chilvers, launched a strange looking craft at Hayling Island, England. It consisted of a hull made from plywood, a universal joint connecting the mast to the hull, a two-piece wishbone, and a Bermudan rig. In January, 1984, it was acknowledged by English law as the first sailboard, and Peter Chilvers was recognised as the inventor of windsurfing! The implications of this judgement are staggering.

Schweitzer's patent in the UK is no longer valid. All British board manufacturers who had a license can now tear it up, and will no longer have to pay the 7½ % royalty. The market is now wide open to everyone, from the small custom board builder, to the big brand name companies. This sudden increase in competition can only be a good thing for the sport, and every windsurfer will benefit. Similar judgements are expected in other countries covered by Schweitzer's patent, and then everyone involved in the sport can get on with the business of having fun.

Olympics Sailboarding is scheduled to be included in the Los Angeles Olympic Games in 1984, the first sport to be included within 15 years of its invention. The board chosen – the Windglider – has been specified to conform with Olympic regulations, and the international Windglider class now has Olympic status.

Board Shapes

It is a tribute to Hoyle Schweitzer's genius that his original Windsurfer is largely unchanged today, and is still considered a good all round sailboard with probably the largest following of one-design racers in the world. When Ten Cate introduced the board to Europe in the early 1970s, its enormous success prompted several manufacturers to produce boards of a similar shape. These boards – of which the Mistral Competition is a good example – became known as flatboards, and, though categorized in Division 1 for racing purposes, are in fact good recreational boards.

Hawaii The next stage in the evolution of board shapes came, not surprisingly, from the now legendary islands of Hawaii. By 1977 two Hawaiian windsurfers – Larry Stanley and Mike Horgan – were having difficulty controlling their boards at high-speed. After experimenting with bigger skegs and re-positioned daggerboards, they discovered that by fitting straps to hold their feet at the back of the board, they had a greater control of the board and could hold it in a straight line at speed. At roughly the same time other windsurfers were exploring the thrill of jumping waves. On a strapless board this technique was confined to bailing out at the top of a jump, as it was not possible to control the board in the air. With footstraps the windsurfer could control the flight and landing of the board, and continue sailing to the next wave. A further advantage was the ability to travel out through the white water, and control the board while riding the waves back in.

The Kailua Kids – as they became known – soon persuaded Schweitzer to modify some of his production Windsurfers. By relocating the daggerboard well and the mast step, fitting footstraps, and adding an extra fin at the back, the world's first 'fun board' was born – the Windsurfer Rocket.

Displacement boards In Europe, with its large following of serious

The first 'funboards' to gain favour in Europe, had very wide, round, tails (left). Some were even shaped like an egg. The wide area of the tail, made them suitable for jumping 'chop' and small waves.

By modern standards, they were far too thick in the tail, which made it very difficult to sink the rails in tight turns, but they had plenty of buoyancy, and were very easy to uphaul. They were, to all intents and purposes, good 'transition' boards.

Development of funboard shapes *The original Windsurfer (1), still regarded today as a good all round sailboard, and (2) a modern all round funboard. At the other, more extreme, end of the funboard range, the early 'European funboard' (3) with its wide, round, and humpbacked tail, and (4) today's definitive funboard, the sinker.*

Board Shapes

triangle racers, manufacturers soon realized that a better board shape was needed to increase speed and win races. This was achieved by creating a 'V' at the front of the hull, and increasing the length of the waterline. At first the rear of the hull was kept flat for stability, and the first of the semi-displacement boards – such as the Hi-Fly III – started getting good results on the racing circuit. Because of the importance of upwind performance in triangle racing, the designers started to concentrate more on the rounded hull shape that pointed upwind so well. These full blown 'formula one' racing models started to look more like canoes than sailboards, and were known as full displacement boards. They were made to conform to the IYRU (International Yacht Racing Union) Division 2 rules for use in Open Class racing. Despite their huge volume – around 85 gals (320 liters) as opposed to the 58 gals (220 liters) of a flatboard – their weight was kept down to the 40 lb (18 kg) minimum by a hollow production method. The result was a very expensive, fragile, board that had outstanding upwind performance in light to moderate winds, but was very unstable and difficult to handle. A prime example of this racing machine is the Mistral M1, which dominated Open Class racing between 1979 and 1982.

The Pan Am Cruiser It became the policy of the major European manufacturers to have their own board designer based in Hawaii, with its excellent testing facilities throughout the year, and its exotic appeal for their advertising copy-writers. The Hawaiians were also keen on racing,

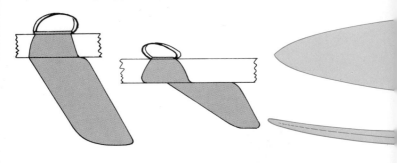

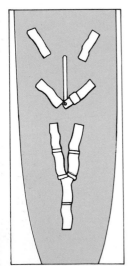

Windsurfer daggerboards
In the search for better performance in high winds, the Windsurfer high wind daggerboard (above), was developed. In comparison with the standard Windsurfer daggerboard (above left), it has a much smaller area that is positioned further back, while it uses the same daggerboard well.

Mistral Pan Am A good example of a production racing board (above), developed from the custom boards used in Pam Am-type racing.

Windsurfer Rocket
The first footstrap board (left). The straps were developed by the Kailua Kids – Larry Stanley and Mike Horgan.

but displacement boards were unsuitable for the high wind racing, often in surf and ocean swells, that they were enjoying. The most famous of these racing events is the Pan Am Cup. From this sometimes gruelling event has evolved a new breed of board, known as the Pan Am Cruiser. This is a high-speed flatboard with a narrow tail, high rocker, numerous footstraps, retractable daggerboard and sliding mast track.

The Funboard The most important recent development in board shape has once again come from the Hawaiian windsurfers. In their quest for boards that will go faster, jump higher and be more maneuverable, they have turned the sport upside-down and created what the European manufacturers have christened the 'funboard'. These originally had square, humpback, tails and semi-retractable daggerboards, which were soon replaced by the 'egg' shaped board with its wide, round tail, more popular in Europe for 'wave hopping'. As manufacturers realized the new marketing potential in this area, 'all round funboards' appeared. These streamlined flatboards were a more stable, tuned down, version of the Pan Am boards. They could be used to learn on, and were still fun in stronger winds when their owners became more competent.

Finally, board design has gone full circle and the board most people want to aspire to now is the 'sinker'. This is a short, light, radically shaped board which looks like a surf-board. Its very thin profile and lack of buoyancy requires it to be planing in at least a Force 4 wind for it to remain afloat. It is the definitive funboard.

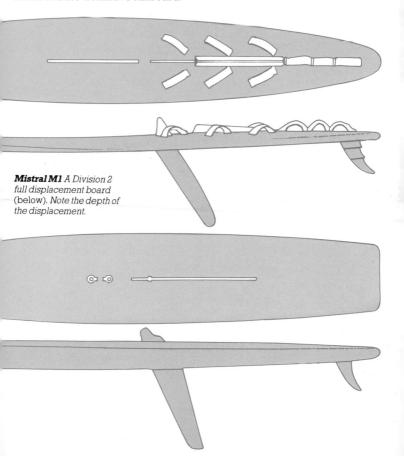

Mistral M1 A Division 2 full displacement board (below). Note the depth of the displacement.

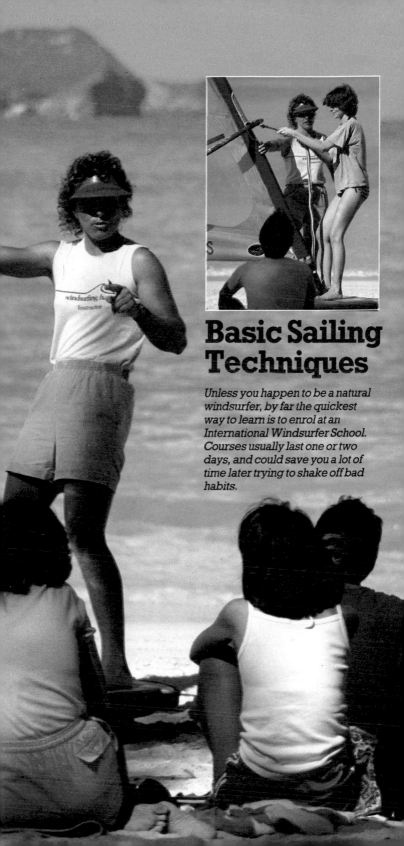

Basic Sailing Techniques

Unless you happen to be a natural windsurfer, by far the quickest way to learn is to enrol at an International Windsurfer School. Courses usually last one or two days, and could save you a lot of time later trying to shake off bad habits.

The Board and Rig

1 Nose or bow.
Sometimes fitted with a rubber bumper and towing eye.
2 Tail or stern.
3 Skeg or fin.
Used singularly, or in triangular formations.
4 Daggerboard.
Sometimes made to retract into the hull.
5 Footstraps.
Fitted in several configurations.
6 Mast foot well.
Often allowing two positions. An alternative is a sliding mast track.
7 Daggerboard well.
Reinforced and built into the hull.
8 Mast or spar.
Made from fiberglass or aluminum, with a single or double taper.
9 Mast foot and universal joint. Made to lock into well, or release under tension.
10 Boom or wishbone.
Fixed or variable length.
11 Sail clew.
Reinforced with metal eyelet.
12 Outhaul. Sometimes used with a pulley system, and tied off with a cleat on the boom.
13 Boom front end.
Often with grip handle.
14 Inhaul. Tied off with a cleat.
15 Uphaul. Knotted to give grip. Hawaiian type is soft with elasticated core.
16 Shock-cord. For use with regular uphaul.
17 Downhaul. Sometimes used with a pulley system, and tied off with a cleat on the mast foot.
18 Safety cord. Joins the mast foot to the board.
19 Battens. Fitted into batten pockets.
20 Leech of the sail.
21 Foot of the sail.

22 Luff of the sail.
23 Mast sleeve.
24 Head of the sail.
25 Mast head.
26 Streamer.
27 Sail number.
28 Class insignia.
29 Tack of the sail.

Plan view (above) The positioning of the footstraps, mast wells, and daggerboard case, is a primary consideration in board manufacture.

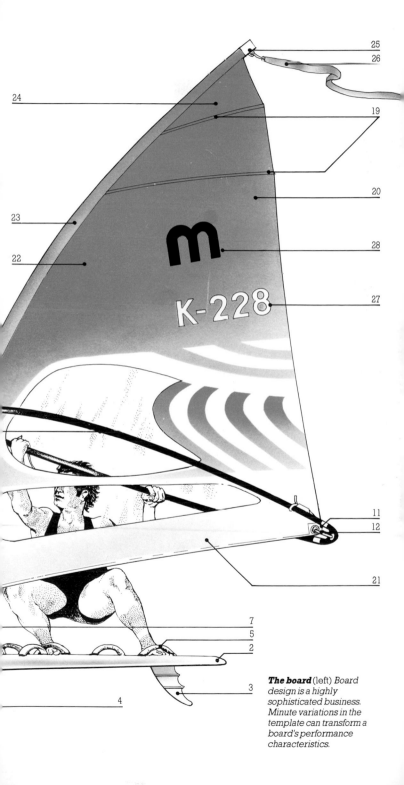

25
26
24
19
20
23
28
22
27
11
12
21
7
5
2
3
4

The board (left) Board design is a highly sophisticated business. Minute variations in the template can transform a board's performance characteristics.

Carrying the Rig

Rigging Up

Carrying the rig Carrying a fully assembled rig down the beach (left) can be quite a handful, especially on a windy day, but it is by no means impossible. One of the easiest and most convenient ways is to carry the rig above your head, supporting it by the boom and mast. Try to keep the front of the boom and the luff of the sail pointing into the wind. This will let the wind pass on either side of the sail, making it much easier to carry.

Rigging up Far too many windsurfers fail to give the rigging up procedure the attention it needs. Although it is relatively simple, it must be done thoroughly not least in the interests of safety. Any equipment failures at sea are dangerous, and it is foolish to increase the risk of one by sailing with an incorrectly assembled rig.

Always check all knots to make sure they are secure – re-tying a knot at sea can be difficult. Double-check all tensioning points, such as the downhaul, uphaul, inhaul, and outhaul, and the battens. But above all take your time, and do not go sailing until you are satisfied that the rig is correctly assembled.

Assembling the Rig

One of the biggest attractions of windsurfing has always been the simplicity of rigging up. While most dinghy sailors are still on the beach fiddling about with a complicated rig, the windsurfer can be on the water and sailing within minutes of arrival.

To rig up, first find a clear space on the shore, making sure it is free of tar. Take the sail out of its bag, and slide the mast into the mast sleeve, narrow end first.

Mast foot Next slide the mast foot assembly into the bottom of the mast, taking care to keep it free of sand, which can cause damage, and will prevent it from locking into the board.

Downhaul Attach the downhaul by passing the line through the tack of the sail, and back to the mast eye. Secure it with a half hitch. Some mast feet have cleats, in which case the downhaul should be passed through it and finished with a half hitch. Try and get as much tension into the downhaul as possible.

Boom height To find the correct height, stand the mast upright. A good

The quickest way to fix the inhaul, is to tie a noose and slip it round the mast at the required height. The distance of the knot from the mast must be found by trial and error.

Lie the boom parallel to the mast and slip the knot into the slot in the boom end. As you lower the boom to the horizontal position, the knot tightens and holds the boom in position.

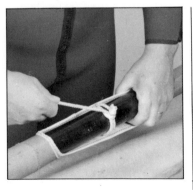

An alternative to the noose, is to tie the inhaul line to the mast at the required height, leaving enough line free to tie the boom with.

Take the line through the boom front eyes and back round the mast, before securing it in the inhaul cleat.

guide to begin with is nose height, but it is more important to choose a height you feel comfortable with.

Inhaul There are two ways of tying the inhaul, which attaches the boom to the mast, the noose method, and the conventional method.

Battens If your sail has battens, insert them now. As you push them to the end of their pockets, they slot into an elastic cup, which allows them to go past their normal position and then reverse into a pocket at the leech end.

Outhaul Tie the outhaul by passing it through the clew of the sail, and tensioning it at the boom outhaul cleat. Lash it tight with a couple of half hitches.

Uphaul Fit the uphaul with a simple knot through the boom front, and a clip on the shock-cord to the downhaul.

Checking Finally, check the tension of the downhaul and outhaul, and stand the complete rig on the beach to see if it looks and feels right. Do not forget to remove any sand from the mast foot before inserting it in the board.

If you find tensioning the outhaul difficult, give yourself a double purchase by passing the outhaul line through the clew eyelet twice.

Some battens need to be tied at the leech end, or may have clips or Velcro straps. It is important to have them correctly tensioned.

Tie knots in the uphaul at regular intervals. These will give you handholds when uphauling.

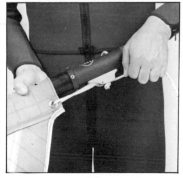

Always give the downhaul tension a final check, and correct it as necessary.

Launching

It is surprisingly easy to break equipment while launching, even in the smallest of waves. Always a tricky maneuver, it can, however, be accomplished quite easily with a little practice. Although it looks easier, it is not always a good idea to take the rig and board into the water separately. Trying to attach the mast foot amid breaking waves is difficult, and can be dangerous. It is generally better to connect the rig to the board while still on the beach. The whole assembly, with the rig to leeward, can be dragged into the water by carrying the front of the board under one arm while holding the boom front with the other.

Landing

On nearing the shore raise the daggerboard, and dismount to windward while keeping hold of the mast. Lift the tail of the board and push it up onto the beach.

Having cleared the water, walk the tail round so that the board now faces backward up the beach. At the same time the wind will swing the rig round so that it flaps freely.

Still holding the tail of the board, support the rig by the boom and drag the two backward up the beach.

Uphauling

Uphauling to leeward Before going sailing, practice uphauling the rig on the beach. Position the board at right angles to the wind, with the rig lying to leeward. Step onto the board with one foot either side of the mast foot, take hold of the uphaul, and move into a squatting position.

Gradually straighten your legs and back while simultaneously pulling on the uphaul.

Continue pulling on the uphaul until the sail begins to clear the water. This is initially very hard work, due to the amount of water lying on top of the sail.

As the water runs off the sail and out of the mast sleeve, uphauling becomes much easier. Keep pulling and moving your hands up the uphaul.

Take hold of the top of the uphaul with one hand, allowing the sail to flap in the wind. When uphauling on the water you will find that as the sail clears the water, the board will begin to move.

Take hold of the top of the uphaul with your other hand, still allowing the sail to flap in the wind. This is the neutral stationary position. When on the water, the board will stop moving as the clew comes out of the water.

Uphauling to Windward

Uphauling to windward *When you fall in, the chances are that the sail will end up to windward of the board. To practice uphauling in this situation, position the board at right angles to the wind, with the rig lying to windward. Start uphauling as before.*

As the sail comes clear the wind will swing it round. Still holding the uphaul, allow the sail to swing, and balance it with your body-weight.

With the sail swinging over the nose of the board, begin to move your feet across the center line, to a position on the windward side.

Let the sail swing onto the leeward side, while your feet balance the board.

With the sail flapping freely on the leeward side, take up the windward feet positions.

Move both hands to the top of the uphaul, thus putting the board into the neutral stationary position.

Getting under Way

Having mastered the neutral position, you are now ready to start sailing, but it is a good idea to practice this procedure on the beach first.

In a light wind, your front foot should be level with, or just in front of, the mast, pointing slightly toward the nose of the board.

Hold the uphaul at the top, by the boom end, with your rear hand, so that the sail is clear of the water.

With your front hand, reach over the top of the 'uphaul hand' to grasp the boom about 8 in (20 cm) from the mast.

Now let go of the uphaul, and hold the neutral position with just your front hand on the boom. The board should not rotate during this maneuver.

With your front, or 'mast hand', pull the mast across the board in front of you, and with your rear, or 'sail hand', grasp the boom about 24 in (61 cm) from the mast hand. Pull the sail hand in, while keeping the mast inclined toward the direction in which you are sailing. This is called 'sheeting in'.

Balancing the sail As you sheet in and the sail fills with wind, you will find yourself being pulled, with the sail, to leeward. To counter this you must lean backward (right), using your body-weight to keep the sail upright. The stronger the force of the wind on the sail, the further you will have to lean back.

Rotating the Board

Rotating the board *You
will often find that having
uphauled the rig, the board
will be facing in the wrong
direction. To turn it, hold
the sail in the neutral
position (left), and slowly
rotate the board through
180° by shuffling it round
with your feet. The rig
should remain in exactly
the same position
throughout the maneuver.*

Stopping

Stopping Learning to stop, preferably in a controlled and elegant manner, is just as important as learning how to start sailing.

To stop the board when under way (left), change your hand positions, so that your mast hand is holding the mast below the boom end, and your sail hand is holding the boom near the mast (below)

Let go of the boom with your rear hand, and take hold of the mast near your front hand. Allow the rig to fall away from you (right) while at the same time squatting down onto the board. With the rig completely in the water, the board will stop (below).

A good sailing stance is the key to a successful windsurfing technique. Always keep your back straight and your knees slightly bent. As the wind strength increases, you must lean back to counterbalance the pull on the sail. Try to be relaxed while at the same time alert to gusts and changes in wind direction, sheeting in and out as necessary. If you sense that the wind is getting too strong for you, let go of the boom and take hold of the uphaul.

It is important to keep the board flat on the water, by keeping your weight in the center and not on the leeward or windward rails. Likewise, you must not stand too far forward, as the board will nosedive into the oncoming waves. As your technique improves and the wind gets stronger, stand further back on the board.

The key to efficient windsurfing is correct weight distribution and balance. If you find yourself straining, you have most probably got a bad stance.

Sailing Theory

A sail behaves in much the same way as an aeroplane wing. Wind flows past either side of the wing and generates lift. Likewise, when the wind hits a sail it separates to pass on either side, and is accelerated on the leeward side by the curve of the sail, causing a reduction in pressure. The greater pressure from the windward side pushes the sail towards the low pressure area, producing 'lift' in a horizontal direction, roughly at right angles to a line between the mast and clew, known as the 'chord' of the sail. To transform this horizontal energy into a driving force that will propel the sailboard forward, a daggerboard is used. Boards that do not have daggerboards work in a slightly different way, but the principle is the same.

Points of sailing (below)
When learning, it is very important that you practice each point of sailing, so that in any given situation you can sail back to the safety of the shore.

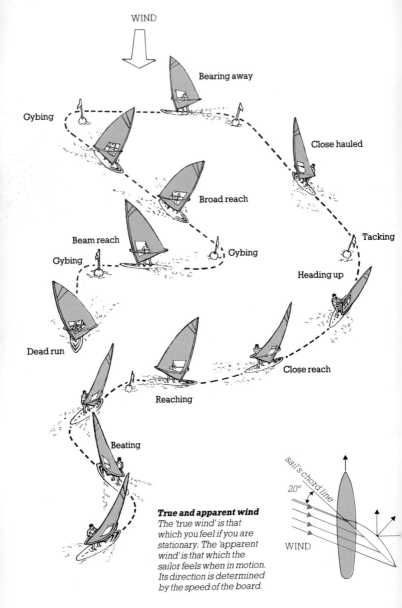

WIND

Bearing away

Gybing

Close hauled

Broad reach

Beam reach

Gybing

Gybing

Tacking

Heading up

Dead run

Close reach

Reaching

Beating

True and apparent wind
The 'true wind' is that which you feel if you are stationary. The 'apparent wind' is that which the sailor feels when in motion. Its direction is determined by the speed of the board.

sail's chord line

20°

WIND

Steering Theory

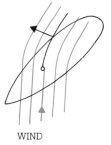

WIND

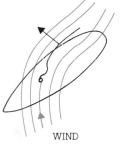

WIND

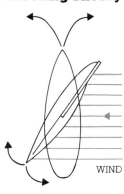

WIND

WIND

Chord line angle The most efficient sailing position is where the sail's chord line is at an angle of 20° to the 'apparent wind'. If the angle is too small the sail will luff and the leeward airflow will lose contact in places, and reduce the pressure difference. If the angle is too great, the leeward airflow will be disturbed and the air leaving the sail will create turbulence. This causes a loss of pressure, and thus a reduced driving force.

Heading up Tilting the rig backward, causes the bow to turn up into the wind.

Bearing away Tilting the rig forward, causes the bow to turn away from the wind.

Centre of effort A sailboard is steered by tilting the rig forward and backward. The 'center of effort' (CE) is the point at which the main force of the wind acts on the sail. This force has a sideways effect, to counteract which it is necessary to have a daggerboard. The daggerboard is the 'center of lateral resistance' (CR).

When the CE is vertically above the CR the board travels in a straight line. When the sail is tilted forward the CE moves forward and the CR acts as a pivot in the water,

forcing the bow downwind. Conversely, as the sail is tilted back the CE goes vertically behind the CR and the stern is pushed to leeward, causing the board to luff up to windward.

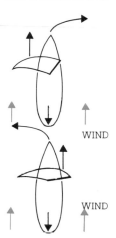

WIND

WIND

Heading Up

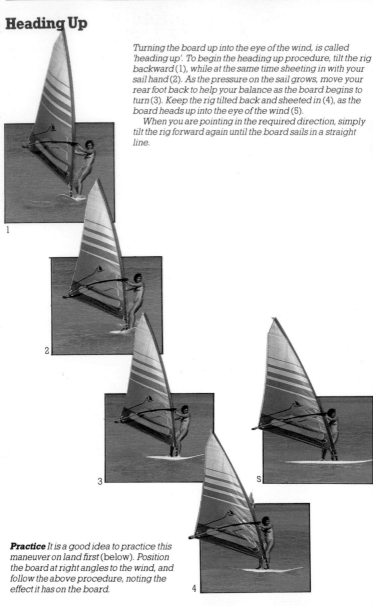

Turning the board up into the eye of the wind, is called 'heading up'. To begin the heading up procedure, tilt the rig backward (1), while at the same time sheeting in with your sail hand (2). As the pressure on the sail grows, move your rear foot back to help your balance as the board begins to turn (3). Keep the rig tilted back and sheeted in (4), as the board heads up into the eye of the wind (5).

When you are pointing in the required direction, simply tilt the rig forward again until the board sails in a straight line.

Practice It is a good idea to practice this maneuver on land first (below). Position the board at right angles to the wind, and follow the above procedure, noting the effect it has on the board.

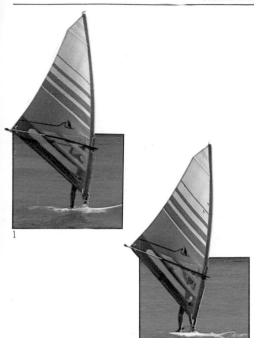

1

2

Bearing Away

Turning the board away from the eye of the wind, is called 'bearing away'. To begin the procedure, tilt the rig forward, while at the same time sheeting in with your sail hand (1). As the pull on the sail changes from the side to the front, move your front foot forward (2), and sheet out with your sail hand (3). The board will now bear away onto a run (4). When you are pointing in the required direction, simply tilt the rig back again until the board sails in a straight line.

3

4

Practice *Try this maneuver out on the beach first (below), until you get the feel of it.*

Tacking

In order to reach a point upwind, you need to sail a zigzag course known as 'tacking to windward'. This is achieved by coming about from a starboard tack to port tack alternately. It is a good idea to practice this maneuver on land first (1). Start by heading up (2), tilting the rig right back (3). Take hold of the uphaul and move in front of the mast (4). Incline the rig to windward to keep up board speed (5), and move to the other side of the sail as the board passes through the eye of the wind (6). Take hold of the boom with your front hand (7), bring the sail across your body (8), and sheet in with your sail hand (9). This completes the tack, and you are now in a position to sail a new course.

1

9

8

7

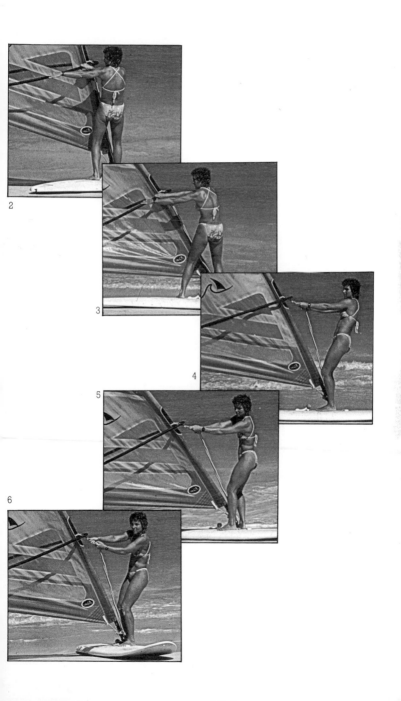

Tacking

Begin your tack by heading up (1), tilting the mast right back (2). Imagine you are trying to dip the clew in the water by bringing it across the board to windward (3), the same side on which you are standing. The board will turn until it is pointing dead into the wind. Then, while letting go of the boom with your sail hand and taking hold of the top of the uphaul, move your feet round in front of the mast, and let go with your mast hand (4). Try to keep the board moving by inclining the rig to windward (5). Once the board has passed through the eye of the wind (6), and is beginning to point in the new direction, move to the other side of the sail, reach over with your free hand and take hold of the boom (7). Bring the sail across your body and sheet in with your sail hand (8), thus completing the tack (9). This stage of the maneuver is the same as that for starting from the neutral position.

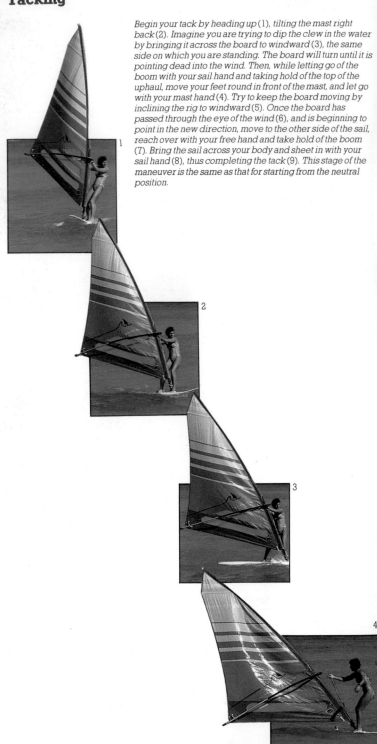

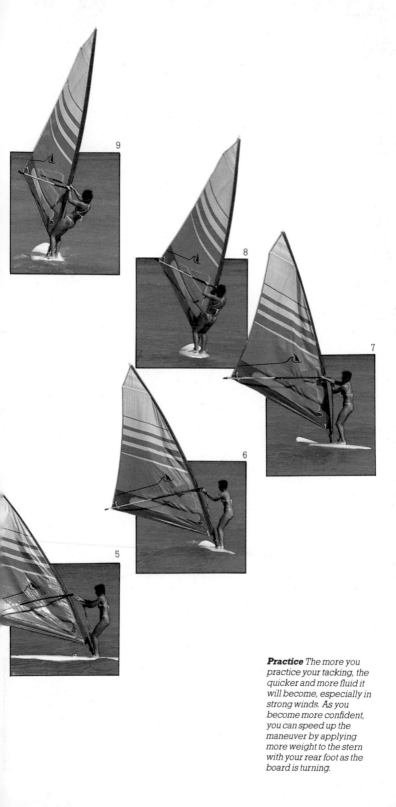

Practice The more you practice your tacking, the quicker and more fluid it will become, especially in strong winds. As you become more confident, you can speed up the maneuver by applying more weight to the stern with your rear foot as the board is turning.

Gybing

Gybing on land The opposite of a tack is a gybe. This is where the board bears away downwind, and the stern, rather than the bow, turns through the eye of the wind. It is a good idea to practice it on land first, before trying it out on the water.

To start the gybe, bear away onto a beam reach (1). Continue to tilt the mast forward (2) while sheeting in with your sail hand. This will push the bow downwind, to leeward. Then, let out your sail hand (3) and move your feet into a position either side of the

daggerboard case (4), as the board begins to point directly downwind. You are now on a run (5), standing square on the board facing forward.

To continue the gybe, let go with your mast hand and grasp the boom front. Then, let go with your sail hand (6) and allow the wind from behind to rotate the sail, clew first, round the mast (7). This will make the bow turn. You then simply reach over with your new mast hand (8) and take hold of the boom, let go of the boom front, grasp the boom

with your new sail hand (9), tilt the mast forward a little and sheet in with your sail hand (10). This completes the gybe.

Gybing

5

6

7

8

9

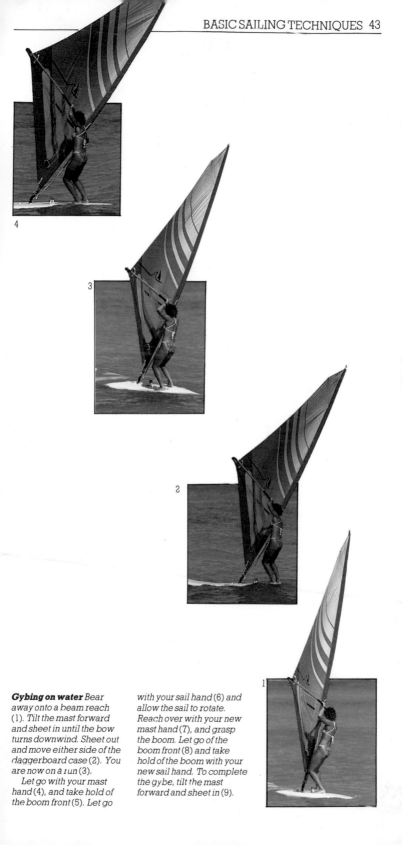

Gybing on water Bear away onto a beam reach (1). Tilt the mast forward and sheet in until the bow turns downwind. Sheet out and move either side of the daggerboard case (2). You are now on a run (3).

Let go with your mast hand (4), and take hold of the boom front (5). Let go with your sail hand (6) and allow the sail to rotate. Reach over with your new mast hand (7), and grasp the boom. Let go of the boom front (8) and take hold of the boom with your new sail hand. To complete the gybe, tilt the mast forward and sheet in (9).

Flare Gybe

This maneuver is a more advanced
version of the standard gybe, and it is often
used in tight situations where several
sailors are trying to round a buoy in a race.
Slow the board down by standing on the
tail. Put pressure on the windward rail to
speed up the turn (above), until the board is
sailing clew first (right). Transfer your sail
hand onto the mast, and let the sail flip.
Sheet in, and then sail away (below).

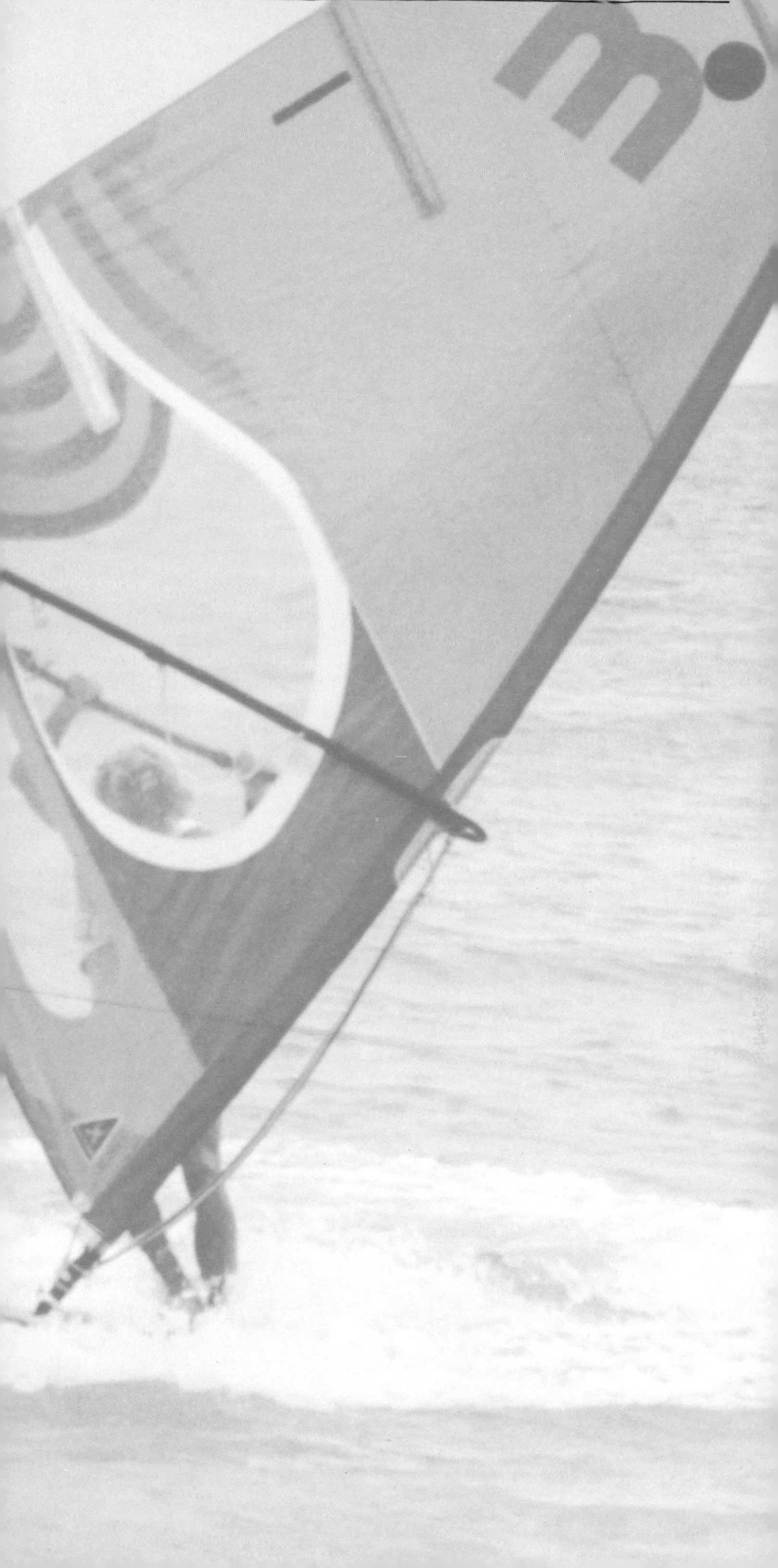

Clothing

After your board, the single most important piece of equipment you will need is a good wetsuit. Wherever you sail, no matter what the prevalent weather conditions are, you will sooner or later have to wear one. A wetsuit is a skintight suit usually made from neoprene, and sometimes lined with nylon or Lycra to give it strength. It works by trapping a thin layer of water between the suit and your body. This is heated up by your body temperature and acts as an insulating layer. In addition, the neoprene itself has a very high insulating capability, due to its synthetic polymer construction.

Choosing a wetsuit When choosing a wetsuit make sure it is a good fit. If you happen to be an unusual shape, several good manufacturers offer a made-to-measure service. The suit should be tight, but not so tight that it constricts your movements. This is particularly important in the case of the arms, where an ill-fitting suit can cause muscle cramp. For this reason the arms are often made from a thinner material than the body, where most of the heat is lost. In the case of a winter suit, commonly called a steamer, this might be a ³⁄₁₆ in (5 mm) body with ⅛ in (3 mm) arms. Summer suits are normally made of thinner neoprene, and come in a variety of styles.

Drysuits An alternative to the winter wetsuit is the drysuit. These were originally made from waterproofed nylon, and were generally bulky and susceptible to leaks. The initial sweating problems were partially over-come by the use of 'breathing' materials such as gortex, which allowed the body to breathe, while preventing water from penetrating the material. They had rubber seals at the neck and wrists, while the feet were enclosed in rubber socks. It was possible to wear thermal underwear beneath the suit for extra warmth.

While many of the problems of conventional drysuits have now been

Swim-suit   Shortie   Long john   Steamer

Gloves *Windsurfing gloves are vital for cold weather sailing. Made from neoprene and leather, and with reinforced palms, they will allow you to sail throughout the year. Lightweight summer gloves are a good idea if your hands suffer from an abrasive boom grip.* **Boots** *Even if your board has a non-slip surface, windsurfing boots can give you extra grip, and will protect your feet when sailing in a rocky environment. However, they may impair 'feel' on short boards. One alternative is the lightweight 'shoe'. These are designed solely to improve grip, and do not have any built-in insulation.* **Buoyancy aids** *A buoyancy aid is not a life-jacket. Most will only float you face down, but will save your strength if you fall in a lot.*

Dry suit Freetex dry suit Two-piece wet-and -dry suit

Seamanship, Safety, and Weather

overcome, they still remain cumbersome, especially when riding short boards in high winds and on waves. One alternative is the watertight 'wetsuit'. Made from blind stitched neoprene, with rubber seals, a waterproof zip, and possibly gortex arms, the suit will keep you warm and comfortable in anything but the worst conditions.

A more recent innovation is the two-piece drysuit, or wet-and-dry suit. This is a 'long john', blind stitched wetsuit, which can be used in the summer but can also be fitted by a waist seal to a gortex pullover top for winter use. Points to watch for when buying a drysuit are: How waterproof is it? Is it easy to get on and off? Do you need help? How warm is it? How easy is it to swim in? Does it interfere with your harness?

Self help A beginner should not venture out in winds over Force 3, or when there is an offshore wind. However, if you do drift out to sea and cannot sail back to shore, *never* leave your board. It will keep you afloat and out of the water, and will lessen the chances of hypothermia, a condition of exposure leading to unconsciousness and eventual drowning. If you need to paddle the board back, do not attempt it with the rig intact, but roll it up in the following manner. Sit on the board, detach the rig, and push it out into the water to windward until you are able to untie the sail at the clew. Then, roll the sail up as tightly as possible along the line of the bottom of the sail to the clew, tucking in any battens as you go. Fold back the boom still attached. Use the downhaul and outhaul to tie the sail to the boom. Then kneel on top of the rig on the deck and start paddling.

Seamanship The rules of seamanship apply not only to windsurfers but to all types of craft. However, it is not recommended that you try to exercise the starboard rule over a supertanker on a port tack. Commercial craft have right of way over pleasure craft. It would be unfair of you to expect a large pleasure yacht to tack out of your way when you could change direction very simply in seconds. Always stay well away from people who are racing, they have right of way over others just cruising around, and can often be unpleasant if you get in their way.

Safety Safety on the water is largely a matter of common sense, so make sure you use it! Follow these basic rules and enjoy your windsurfing. Find out about weather conditions. Ask a local about the presence of currents, reefs, etc. See if there are any rescue facilities. Have someone keep an eye on you. Learn your right of way. Check your equipment for wear and tear. Make sure you are wearing the right clothing. Take out third party insurance.

Weather Every sailor should have some understanding of the weather, and in particular the wind. Wind is created by a pressure differential. As the sun heats up the land, the air above it rises and creates a low pressure

The Beaufort Scale

Force 0		Calm.	Mirror like sea.
Force 1	1 – 3 knots.	Light air.	Gentle ripples.
Force 2	4 – 6 knots.	Light breeze.	Small wavelets.
Force 3	7 – 10 knots.	Gentle breeze.	Large wavelets.
Force 4	11 – 16 knots.	Moderate breeze.	Small waves. Some white horses.
Force 5	17 – 21 knots.	Fresh breeze.	Moderate waves. Many white horses.
Force 6	22 – 27 knots.	Strong breeze.	Large waves. White crests, some spray.
Force 7	28 – 33 knots.	Near gale.	Sea heaps up. Foam from breaking waves blows in streaks.
Force 8	34 – 40 knots.	Gale.	Moderately high waves. Edge of crests break into spindrift.
Force 9	41 – 47 knots.	Strong Gale.	High waves. Crests of waves breaking and toppling over. Spray may effect visibility.
Force 10	48 – 55 knots.	Storm.	High waves. Long overhanging crests. Sea surface becomes white.

Seamanship *A board on starboard tack – when the wind is coming from the starboard side* (right), *has right of way over a board on port tack. Remember, if your right hand is at the front of the boom it is your right of way. When two boards are on the same tack* (below), *the windward board (ie the board nearest the direction of the wind) must keep clear of the leeward board. A board tacking or gybing (below right) must keep clear of one that is not.*

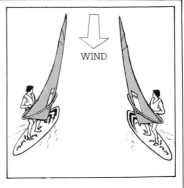

Distress *The International Distress Signal for help* (below) *is to raise your arms above your head and wave them from side to side. It is important to do this correctly so that it is obvious that you are in distress and not simply waving.*

Self help *It is a good idea to practice the dismantling and paddling back technique* (above), *so that the first time you really need to use it you know what to do.*

area. This draws in the cooler air from over the sea, resulting in an onshore wind. As the sun goes down, the land cools and the reverse happens, resulting in an offshore wind. 'High' pressure areas are generally settled with light to moderate winds. 'Low' pressure areas are the opposite, with unsettled weather and strong to stormy winds. The wind generally blows from the high to the low pressure area, and its strength, which is determined by the difference in pressure, is measured in millibars.

You can get information about the weather from television and radio broadcasts, but it is worth ringing your local weather center to get more precise details concerning the strength and direction of the wind at the coast. They will quote you the wind strength in units of *Force*. This refers to the Beaufort Scale, and is not only related to knots (nautical miles per hour), but also to the effect the wind has on the appearance of the sea.

Funboards

By the beginning of 1980, a large number of enthusiastic European windsurfers were becoming increasingly disillusioned with flat water, Olympic triangle, racing. The round bottomed, Division 2, racing boards were difficult to sail, and were not really suitable for high wind racing. It was against this background that funboards really came into their own, with their superb high wind performance, and their suitability for wave sailing.

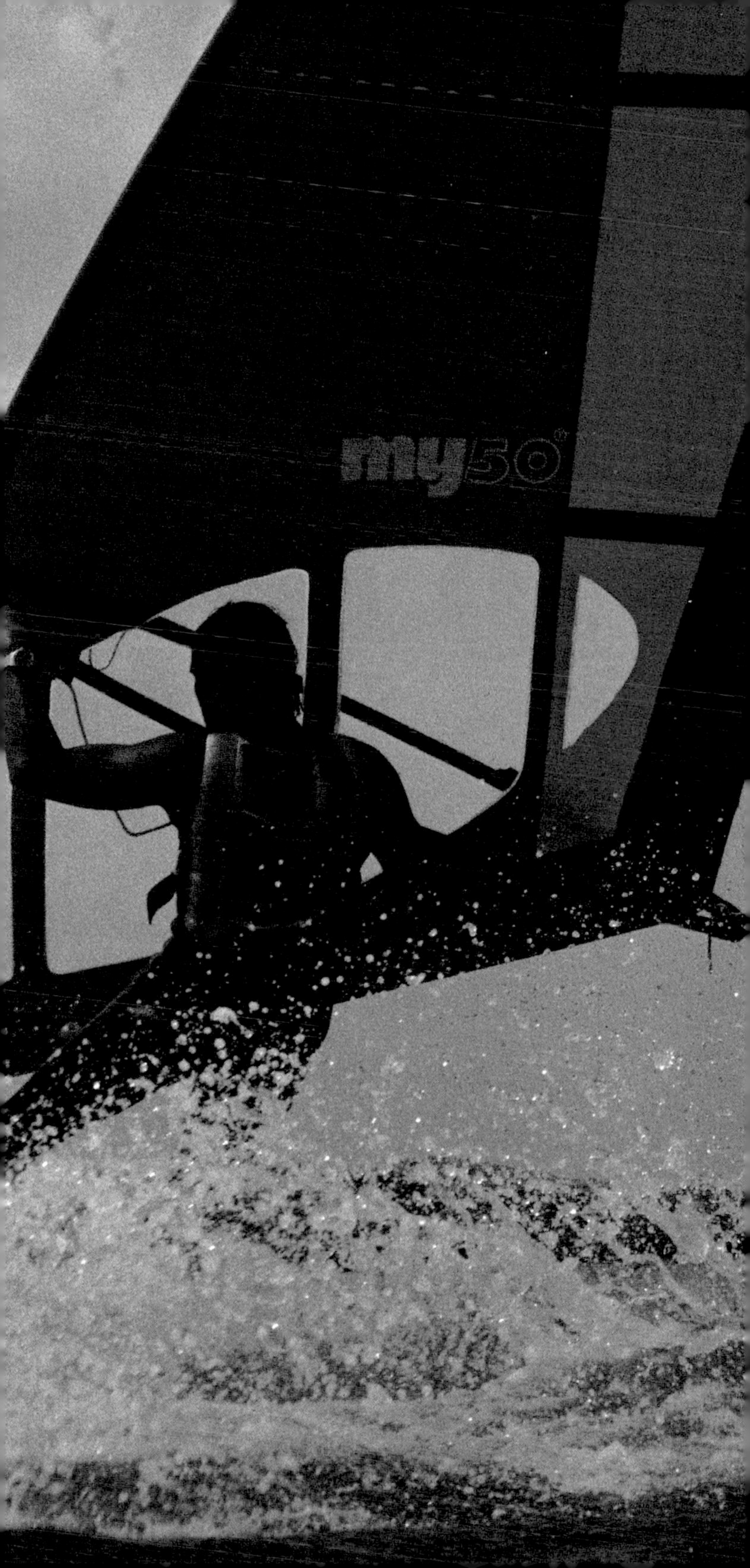
my50

Types of Funboards

All round The board that most average sailors will learn on, and that will be suitable for a beginner up to the intermediate level. Its main performance characteristics are easy handling, and the ability to perform in a wide range of conditions, from light winds and flat water, to strong winds and small waves.

It may come equipped with a sliding mast track, adjustable footstraps, a retractable daggerboard, and a removable skeg. The most commonly used materials for the hull, are a foam core covered with epoxy or plastic. Due to the nature of its general use by beginners and learners, it is designed to be especially durable.

Transition The next step up from the all round board, and in many cases, due to unfavourable conditions, the final step. It has enough buoyancy to support the average sailor while stationary, and can be tacked and uphauled. Its main performance characteristics are the ability to handle light and gale force winds, and to carve turns, while it is manageable on waves and in jumps. However, due to its bulk, performance in the upper level is somewhat limited.

Hull features include removable skegs (usually three), footstraps, thinner rails at the tail, and a variety of tail shapes. Some upper range boards have a retractable daggerboard, and sliding mast track.

Semi-sinker A minimum Force 3 is necessary for this board to start performing. It is designed for high performance gybing, jumping, wave riding, and speed runs. At below planing speeds it is very unstable and difficult to point upwind. Boards of this length do not have daggerboards, and are sailed upwind by keeping the rig sheeted in and raked back, while digging in the windward rail.

Due to the lack of buoyancy, water starts are mandatory, and as there is very little board area in front of the mast foot, tacking is out of the question. When lulls in the wind are encountered the board has enough buoyancy to keep going, (usually with the help of some 'pumping').

Sinker The definitive funboard, it comes into its own in a Force 5 or more. Once water starts and gybing are mastered, it is the easiest and most exciting board to sail, but it does have limitations. It is difficult to sail upwind, and will sink if the wind drops. The mast step is always positioned between 65–70 in (165–178 cm) from the tail.

Most high performance sinkers are custom made, as production boards tend to be too heavy. Research and development in board design is intense, as it has been found that minute variations in tuning can profoundly affect the board's performance, especially on waves. Skeg, footstrap, and mast step positions, combined with rail shapes and the template of the board all determine its ultimate performance.

'Gun' The first 'gun' sailboards were converted Waimea surf-boards. It was found that in a Force 6 or more, the narrow tail planed very flat and held in well in turns. In recent years 'gun' inspired boards have been used with some success at speed trials. (Philip Pudenz held an unofficial world record for a month, of 26.5 knots on a converted Waimea surfboard.) The term 'gun' is now applied to any sinker or semi-sinker sailboard that has a drawn-out outline, and a wide point forward of center. Most boards use a single skeg, and a mast step further forward than usual, roughly 75 in (190 cm) from the tail. All are custom made.

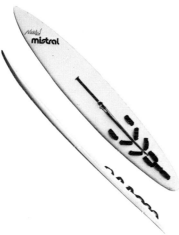

Racing The length of the board, often up to 13 ft (4 m), promotes good upwind performance, while the flat and 'V'-shaped bottom, combined with the pulled-in tail, make planing and carved turns manageable.

Templates vary considerably, and are determined by such factors as the rider's weight, and the conditions the board is to be used in. The most commonly used tail shapes are the pintail and the squashtail. A single skeg, retractable daggerboard, and sliding mast track are all standard equipment, as are an array of up to 11 footstraps. The forward straps are used for beating, and are positioned close to the rails to counteract the hydroplaning tendency of the daggerboard. The rear straps are for downwind work, and are positioned along the center line.

Funboard Size Guide

Sinker (1) *Length 7-8½ft (2.1-2.6m), width up to 22in (56cm).*
Semi-sinker (2) *Length 8-9ft (2.4-2.7m), width up to 24in (60cm).*
Transition (3) *Length 9½-10½ft (2.9-3.2mm), width up to 24½in (61cm).*
Gun (4) *Average measurements, length 9ft (2.7m), width 20in (51cm).*
All round (5) *Length 11-12ft (3.3-3.8m), width up to 25in (62cm).*
Race (6) *Length up to 13ft (4m), width up to 24in (60cm).*

Choosing the Right Funboard

Pop-out or custom The first question facing the potential funboard owner is whether to buy a molded 'pop-out' or a 'custom' board. The advantage of having a custom board 'shaped' for you, is that it will exactly match your particular requirements. However, this presupposes that you know what these requirements are, and this is something that can only be arrived at through extensive windsurfing experience. If you have this, you can then sit down with your 'shaper' and discuss every detail of the board, and how you want it to be. An experienced shaper will be able to tell you whether your ideas are possible, and indeed whether they will result in the required performance – so listen to him!

For the less experienced sailor, it is generally a better idea to buy a 'pop-out' or molded board. This manufacturing process covers all types of boards, from all round funboards to extreme sinkers. They are made from a 'plug', which is the name given to the original custom board from which the mold is taken. The main drawback with this process is that the finer points of the original design are blurred or lost in the mold. The main advantage is, of course, the lower cost.

It is also worth remembering that a molded board made by a reputable manufacturer will most likely be the result of extensive testing by experienced sailors, and it is unlikely to be a bad design. If possible, always test the board yourself before deciding, (something you cannot do with a custom board), and bear in mind that it takes time to adjust to a more advanced board. A board that feels unstable now will feel 'responsive' with a little practice.

Weight Body-weight has a profound effect on board performance. Obviously the heavier you are the more buoyancy you will need, especially when beginning. It should be remembered that custom boards are generally lighter than production boards, although the new molded epoxy/styrofoam process is closing the gap. Excessively heavy boards should be avoided as they lack both jumping and speed performance.

Locations Where you sail is just as important as what you sail. When choosing a new board, think about where you will be doing most of your sailing. Find out what the average wind strength is, and match this to the board specifications. If you sail in the sea and expect to specialize in wave sailing, always be pessimistic about maximum wind speeds, and take this

Sinking *Not enough wind and too much weight, (left) and the board will sink!*

Buying a board *A reputable dealer (right) should be able to advise you on board suitability, and arrange testing facilities.*

***Body-weight/board
volume guide*** *The amount
of buoyancy you need in a
funboard is dependent on
your body-weight. To use
the guide, look in the
section relevant to your
sailing ability, for the point
where your body-weight
line meets the graph line,
and then look below for the
minimum volume required*

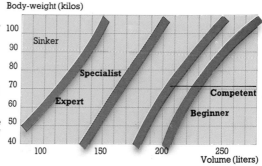

Body-weight (kilos)

Sinker

Specialist

Expert

Competent

Beginner

Volume (liters)

into account when considering buoyancy. If you sail in an area with strong currents, you may need a retractable daggerboard, so do your research *before* buying a board.

Time If you have an unlimited amount of time in which to go sailing, you will probably develop a technique good enough to sail a wide range of boards. However, if your sailing time is limited it is better to opt for a more forgiving board, which will make fewer demands on your technique, than the latest, most radical, custom model.

Cost In the windsurfing world it is always advisable to buy the best available. If you are not buying a custom board, make sure you go to reputable dealers. They will want you to come back in the future, and so are unlikely to sell you a dud. However, they need to make a living and sometimes get stuck with old stock or last year's model, so ask around and compare prices. Find out whether they will accept your old board in part exchange, or your new one when you decide to upgrade. It is also a good idea to buy from someone who knows where you sail. Not only will they be able to advise you on equipment suitable for your local conditions, but most importantly will be able to arrange for you to test it there.

If your finances are limited it is best to opt for a second-hand, well-known board rather than a 'special offer' on an unknown board. A second-hand board will hold its value well, as the first owner will have already taken the initial loss. Always bargain when buying second-hand, and on average offer 30% less than the asking price.

Tail Shapes

Tail profiles are an important factor in board performance. The width and thickness determine how well the board grips in the turn, and the curve determines the radius of the turn.

When carving a turn, the inside rail is depressed, and 'grips' the water. The thinner the rail the easier it is to depress. A wide tail helps the board to plane, and gives lift on jumps, but is difficult to sink at speed for turning. The opposite applies to narrow tails. A curved tail gives the board a shorter turning radius, a straight tail gives it a longer one.

Winged pintail *(4) Wings, normally positioned 1 ft (30.5 cm) from the tip, decrease the area at the very end of the board. This keeps a good planing area beneath the feet, while the small decrease in area behind the wings makes the tail easier to sink in turns, thus making it grip better. It is a good all round tail shape.*

Round pintail *(5) The traditional tail shape, less widely used today, as it is felt that a broken tail outline is preferable. This tail shape has good lift and smooth turning characteristics, and while having no bad points is rather too dependent on suitable conditions.*

Squashtail *(2) This tail shape gives very good lift in marginal conditions, due to its large planing area at the tip of the board. It is suitable for jumping, small wave riding, and is often used on race and slalom boards. Its main drawback is that it is very difficult to sink in fast turns, and often causes spin-outs and slide-outs. It is widely used on surf-boards.*

Swallow-tail *(1) The theory behind this tail shape is that it decreases the tail area on the side being depressed in a turn, as a result of the cut-out shape at the tip of the board. It works very well on surf-boards because they travel at a slower speed, but it is doubtful whether it has much effect on sailboards. It is largely regarded now as a bit of a gimmick.*

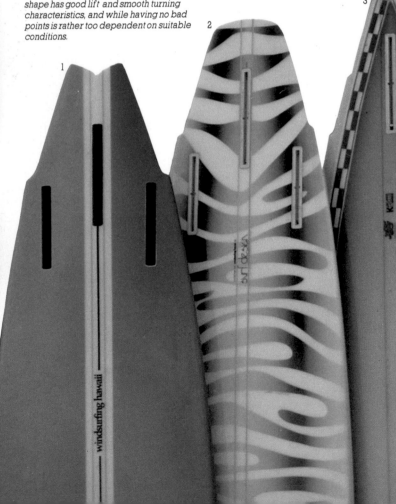

Double wing swallow-tail (3) The double wings help keep the planing area beneath the rider's back foot. The first step is normally 15 in (38 cm) from the tip, behind which the tail gets considerably narrower, making depression in turns much easier. The swallow cut-out at the tip is really only there for show, and does not seriously affect the board's performance. This is one of the most popular tail shapes now used.

Diamond tail Another way of reducing the area at the extreme tip of the board, (so as to improve its high-speed turning capability), the diamond tail is not widely used on sailboards today. Some specialist racing boards do, however, use it. The reason for this unpopularity has more to do with fashion than with any serious design drawbacks.

Funboard Dynamics

Board profiles In recent years, the custom sailboard industry has greatly benefited from the growing involvement of surf-board shapers, who have brought with them years of experience in board design. However, there are significant differences between a surf-board and a sailboard, and it would be unreasonable to expect a 7½ft (2.3 m) surf-board with a mounted rig to perform as well as a sailboard. Unlike a surf-board, a sailboard needs extra volume under the mast step to provide compensatory buoyancy.

The thickness of the board should taper off towards the tail. In order to carve fast, tight turns, the tail needs to be foiled very thin, so that the rider can sink it, and make it bite and grip in the turn. Too much volume in the tail reduces its ability to grip, and this makes carving a gybe extremely difficult, if not impossible.

Scoop and rocker The amount of upturn in the nose and tail, known as the nose rocker (or scoop) and tail rocker, is measured by laying the board on a flat surface.

The scoop helps keep the nose up when the board is not planing, and prevents it nosediving. On short boards it would normally be about 6-7 in (15-18 cm), and on long boards 7-9 in (18-23 cm). It is a gradual upturn, taking up the front section of the board.

The tail rocker influences the turning ability of the board, and takes up the rear section. It is not normally more than 2½ in (6 cm), as too much tail rocker can slow the board down. The amount of tail rocker shaped into the board is critical, but only experience can tell how much is needed to match certain conditions.

Rail shapes As the thickness of the board changes from the nose to the tail, so does the shape of the edges, known as the 'rails'. These changes in rail shape are blended into one another to form a smooth, flowing, uninterrupted line. The quality of the rail shape is an important factor in a board's performance potential.

On a racing board, for example, the rail design could be examined in three sections. The front section would normally have hard rails on the top, and soft rails below, thus forming a displacement bow. The middle section would have soft rails, becoming harder in the foiled out tail section.

Water release On short, wave boards, it is necessary to have a water release edge under the rails, running from the nose to the tail. This hard edge stops the water from wrapping around the rails, and makes the board quicker to plane. Above this edge is a rounded area, known as the 'tuck'. As the board banks in a turn, it comes off the water release edge and goes onto the tuck and sticks, thus improving the turning ability generated, by depressing the leeward rail of the thin tail area.

Underwater profiles There are, today, many different underwater profiles in production, each having a very distinctive set of performance characteristics.

Flat Very quick to plane and very stable, a flat underwater shape is used on most beginner boards in the mast foot area. High performance wave boards also have a flat planing area around the front footstrap positions.

Triplane At below planing speeds, the board displaces water from rail to rail, and when planing, rises onto the flat section. This profile is very stable in strong winds, and due to its longer and narrower wetted area when planing, is less likely to spin-out. It is normally used on boards of 10 ft (3 m) or more.

Round A round underwater profile is used on Open Class racing boards. Known as displacement hulls, they are very fast at below planing speeds, and will point very high upwind. However, these boards are difficult to sail, especially downwind and in choppy seas, and are designed solely for racing.

'V' The tail section of high performance wave boards is shaped into a 'V' to help rail to rail transitions, and promote directional stability. An exaggerated 'V' shape will make the board slow to plane, but very stable while planing. It also enables a much smaller skeg than normal to be used. Some race and slalom boards are shaped with a 'V' running from the nose to the tail, with the maximum depth around the daggerboard case. This helps upwind pointing, and also control while reaching.

Channel hulls Channeled hulls are used to give a board lift, and thereby make it plane quicker. They function quite simply by channeling the air underneath the board.

In the past many shapers were unwilling to work on channeled hulls because of the extra work involved in shaping, glassing, and sanding. The situation has altered recently, as the benefits of such an underwater profile have become more widely recognized. Many of the boards now used in Fun Cup racing incorporate a 'V'-shaped and twin-channeled hull, partly as a response to the light wind conditions the competitions have recently been held in.

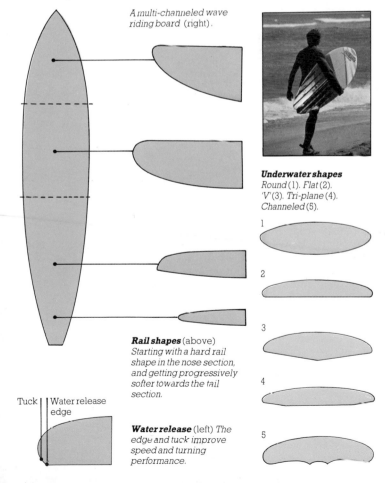

A multi-channeled wave riding board (right).

Underwater shapes
Round (1). *Flat* (2).
'V' (3). *Tri-plane* (4).
Channeled (5).

1

2

3

4

5

Rail shapes (above)
Starting with a hard rail shape in the nose section, and getting progressively softer towards the tail section.

Tuck | Water release edge

Water release (left) *The edge and tuck improve speed and turning performance.*

Fins

Function The function of a fin is to stabilize the board's direction, and to act as a pivot in turns.

US fin box system Polycarbonate boxes (1) are laminated into custom and production boards. The fin is secured by a stainless steel screw (2), into a sliding plate inside the box. This widely used system enables the fin to be replaced easily.

Materials Production fins are usually made from polycarbonate or plastic. Mass production makes them very cheap, but they do suffer from such structural problems as improper foiling, and excessive flexing. Fiberglass custom fins are made from glass mat sandwiched between 14-20 layers of 6 oz (180g) cloth. The laid up sheets are cut, foiled by grinder and sander, and then coated with resin. The foil must be smooth and continuous from the leading to the trailing edge.

Glassed-on fins This is the lightest and most hydrodynamically efficient way of attaching a fin, and it is widely used on surfboards (3). However, due to the stresses involved when a sailboard travels at high speed, this method is only used for small, side, thrusters. Its most serious drawback, is that it causes transportation difficulties, as the fins are permanently fixed.

Cavitation At high speeds, air is drawn down the fin causing it to cavitate, and consequently to lose its tracking ability. When this happens in conjunction with excessive pressure from the back foot on the

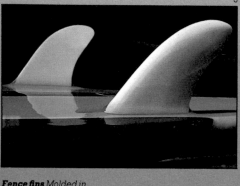

Fence fins Molded in plastic, the function of the two 'fences' is to help prevent air from being sucked down the fin at speed, which causes cavitation. They work very well on narrow-tailed boards, and in conjunction with small thrusters on wide-tailed boards.

tail, the board will tend to spin-out. Narrow boards suffer less than wide boards in this respect, as the longer planing area and greater amount of rail in the water help the board's tracking.

Fins are often blamed for spin-outs, when it is really the rider's bad technique.

Single fins A single fin (4) is widely used on narrow and racing boards, where a very tight turning radius is not necessary. It is also often used on big wave boards.

Tri fins (5) By far the most popular arrangement used today, it facilitates high-speed sailing, with the side fins, or 'thrusters', making up for the lost rail length of a wide-tailed board on a plane. The thrusters must be at least a third of the size of the trailing fin, or they develop a hydroplaning effect in steeply banked turns.

New shapes Research and development constantly produce new shapes (6). However, it takes a season of testing in good conditions to determine their real value.

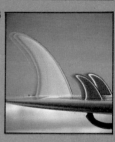

Football fins Introduced by the Hawaiian shaper, Doug Mann, the theory behind them is that cavitation begins at the base of the fin. By reducing the area of the base and increasing the area of the tip, the fin is less prone to cavitation.

Footstraps

Developed in the 1970s by Larry Stanley and Mike Horgan, footstraps were initially designed for wave jumping, but were also found to be useful for high-speed sailing on flat water. Apart from giving an added sense of security, they do improve control of the board and will save your strength in high winds. However, they need to be used carefully, as serious ligament damage can occur if your feet are still in the straps when you fall.

Most modern footstraps consist of a rubber, plastic, or webbing strip attached to the board in a small loop, and covered with a neoprene tube to protect your feet. On wave boards the correct positioning of the footstraps is vital, as the rider needs to be completely in control of the board, when performing complicated moves on wave faces.

One of the many variations of production board fittings (1), permanent and adjustable. (2) a simple screw-in system. Plastic inserts or plugs are glassed into the deck, and the straps are screwed in. Cobra tension-release straps (3) are likewise fitted into glassed-in inserts. This system is very efficient, and under extreme pressure the strap releases, thereby avoiding ligament damage.

The Ten Cate system (4) is a variation on the Cobra principle. The straps are locked into inserts by rotation through 90°, and will break before reaching the stress level required to pull them out of the board. The glassed-in fitting (5,6) can only be used on a foam custom board. A 1 × 2 in (2.5 × 5 cm) deep slot is routed in the board and filled with resin, into which the webbing is inserted.

Single Y *Used on boards under 9½ ft (2.9m), where the feet stay in the same position while planing. The front straps are positioned at an angle of 45° to the center line, and about a shoulder's width from the back strap.*

Double rear *The back rear strap is used for jumping, and the forward one for reaching. The reason for moving the back foot slightly further up the board while going fast, is to put less pressure on the tail and thus reduce the risk of a spin-out.*

Double Y *Normally used on longer boards, and for two reasons. Some have a different strap position for fast and slow planing. And, as a beginner may have difficulty in using the rear straps at first, the front ones serve as 'trainers'.*

Starboard tack wave riding

Port tack jumping

Offsets *Sometimes used on narrow and asymmetrical wave boards, where it is not possible to position the front straps side by side over the center line, or the rear jumping strap. The straps are offset and, by using inserts, the board is suitable for riding waves on both tacks.*

Mistral racing board (below) *The forward straps are used for beating, and the rear straps for downwind work. There are usually between 9 and 11 footstraps on this board.*

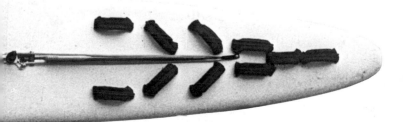

Asymmetrical Shapes

Asymmetrical boards, (ie boards with irregular templates), are essentially high performance wave riding boards. Their development began when it was discovered that the best outlines for 'bottom turns' and 'off-the-lip turns' were different. A number of board shapers began experimenting with different curves on each side of the board, and with some success. Initially the boards had a drawn-out pintail on the bottom turn side, (where the speed of the turn is fastest), and a squashtail on the cutback side, (where the speed of the turn is slowest).

To begin with these boards were regarded as gimmicks, and were not taken seriously until Craig Masonville of Hi Tech Sailboards on Maui, began experimenting with a design nicknamed 'the Can-opener'. This was a board specifically designed for riding big, fast waves, up to one and a half masts high – typical winter conditions on Hookipa. The starboard (bottom turn) side of the board had a drawn-out pintail for fast, controlled turns in the chop. It had a small amount of tail rocker to make it plane flatter and give the rail more bite. The port (cutback) side had a squashtail, with the wide point behind the center, a lot of curve and extra tail rocker, and was 12 in (30.5 cm) shorter. There was also a provision, on the port side, for an extra skeg to help prevent side-slip on cutback turns. The result was a board that made very fast and smooth bottom turns, and extremely tight and 'snappy' cutbacks.

Board development in the asymmetrical field is still very much in its infancy, but there can be no doubt that they are here to stay, and will feature very strongly in the future. However, they do have one serious drawback – they can only be used in locations where there is one wind direction. This is fine if you happen to live on the North Shore of Maui, where the wind always blows from right to left, but if you live elsewhere you will need two boards. Also, it must be said that asymmetricals only really come into their own when there are ideal conditions, with side-shore waves over half a mast high. In choppy conditions it is better to use a conventional board.

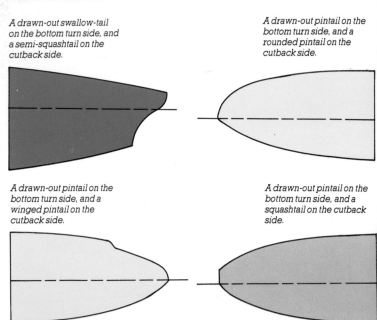

A drawn-out swallow-tail on the bottom turn side, and a semi-squashtail on the cutback side.

A drawn-out pintail on the bottom turn side, and a rounded pintail on the cutback side.

A drawn-out pintail on the bottom turn side, and a winged pintail on the cutback side.

A drawn-out pintail on the bottom turn side, and a squashtail on the cutback side.

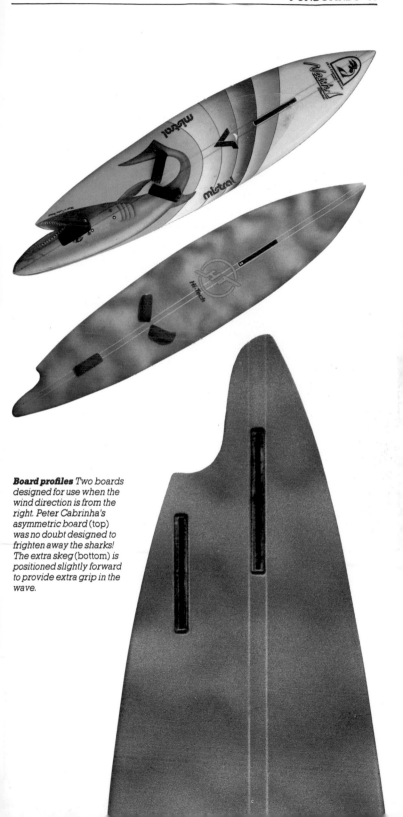

Board profiles Two boards designed for use when the wind direction is from the right. Peter Cabrinha's asymmetric board (top) was no doubt designed to frighten away the sharks! The extra skeg (bottom) is positioned slightly forward to provide extra grip in the wave.

Mast Tracks and Daggerboards

Mast tracks Sliding mast tracks are used on all racing boards so that the position of the mast can be altered while sailing a course. The range of movement is usually between 70–90 in (1.8–2.3 m) from the stern of the board. The track is either fitted onto or recessed into the deck with screw fittings. The mast track assembly consists of a power joint and mast foot, mounted on a runner that slides along an aluminum track. The system is foot operated by means of a catch and rubber bungee cord.

For upwind sailing, the mast should be in the forward position, as a longer wetted surface area of the hull makes the board point better and go faster upwind. It forces the nose down, thus improving performance in light winds, while permitting the sailor to hang his weight on the sail more effectively, which in turn allows him to handle a larger sail. On rounding the weather mark the mast should be pulled aft, thus reducing the wetted area, and relieving the pressure on the nose. This allows the sailor to stand further aft and facilitates efficient downwind planing.

Making final adjustments (1). The shock-cord (2) tensions the runner, as does a rack system (3).

One advantage of having a sliding mast track on an all round funboard, is that if the wind picks up out at sea the sailor stands a better chance of getting back to shore.

Retractable daggerboards The purpose of the daggerboard is to stop the board drifting away from the wind when sailing upwind. It is made to retract, so that when the board is planing downwind it does not cause drag, turbulence, and most importantly, hydroplaning. When a daggerboard hydroplanes it rises to the surface and can cause the board to tip onto its rails or capsize.

The daggerboard is normally positioned some 60–65 in (1.5–1.7 m) from the stern. It is held in position by rubber friction shims, while a protrusion on the top makes it foot operable.

To reduce underwater drag, the daggerboard well has self-closing flaps made from rubber Mylar or Dacron. On racing boards the daggerboard itself is usually made from laminated wood.

Mast feet The proper functioning of the mast foot is vital to the overall performance of the board. In the old days, it consisted of a mechanical double swivel attached to a piece of wood, and was fixed to the board by jamming the wood into a slot. It had a nasty habit of coming out during uphauling, and often caused irritating injuries.

Today's production mast feet have adjustable tension-release mechanisms, and use a power joint instead of a mechanical swivel. Most manufacturers have their own mast foot designs. Some use a locking system, while

Mast Feet and Fin Box Systems

others use the adjustable tension system. Generally speaking, it is better to lock your mast into the board, as you can get into a lot of trouble at sea trying to cope with a mast foot that keeps coming out. It is very important to keep your mast foot free from sand, which not only jams up the system, but also reduces its efficiency, and makes it more likely to come out.

Custom fin box systems The most efficient and the cheapest way to attach the mast foot to a custom board is with a conventional US fin box. On custom wave boards it is vital that the mast foot should never come out, as it can be highly dangerous trying to re-insert the mast foot amid breaking waves.

The fin box allows the mast position to be adjusted when tuning the board for peak performance. The center of the box should be positioned 70 in (1.8 m) from the stern. Moving the mast forward makes the board less easy to turn, but improves its speed. Moving the mast back has the opposite effect.

The very successful Mistral system (1) has since been copied by other manufacturers. One alternative is the adjustable system (2), whereby the male piece is expanded when inserted by rotating the collar.

Double fin box A double fin box should be used on boards with only one stringer. This is necessary because cutting the stringer would seriously weaken the structure of the board, so much so that it could break upon landing after a wave jump. The system is very efficient, but does require the use of a removable mast foot base. For boards with two stringers a single fin box can be used.

Windsurfing Hawaii triangle system The latest in mounting units for custom boards, this consists of a single bolt offset in a triangular base, with a slot routed into the fin box. The plate is inserted through the slot and tightened by rotating the triangular base. The only drawback is that the fin box must be reinforced with at least four layers of 6 oz (180 g) fiberglass, to prevent it shattering.

A standard single fin box (1) and double fin box system (2). The power joint and extension base are attached to a nylon plate, which is then screwed into the plates in the fin box. The triangular unit (3) can be fitted in a few seconds and adjusted easily. A mast pad (4) is vital to protect the deck area around the mast foot from being damaged by the universal joint.

Developments in sail design have kept pace with the ever growing demands of windsurfers. With boards becoming more and more responsive, sail designers have done away with the low aspect, long boom, sail of the past, and introduced high aspect, short boom sails. These computer cut sails, identical to those used in races and wave riding contests in Hawaii, are now mass-produced, and are widely available.

Funboard Sails

History of Funboard Sails

Maui Sails No two people have contributed more to the development and design of today's funboard sails, than Barry Spanier and Geoffrey Bourne of Maui Sails. Finding themselves on the Hawaiian island of Maui in 1979, about the time when people like Mike Waltze began sailing a Windsurfer in the heavy surf at Hookipa, they were in the right place at the right time. Even though the sport was already 10 years old, the development of equipment had been almost negligible, due to the continuing legal wrangles caused by the patent dispute. People were just not willing to invest capital in developing products when there was a serious possibility that they would not be able to sell them. However, in Hawaii there were no one-class rules or restrictions, and none of the problems the European manufacturers were experiencing trying to produce and sell complete boards and rigs. Instead, there was a hardcore of enthusiastic windsurfers eager to improve on the only mass-produced equipment available to them at the time.

Maui Sails was originally set up to deal with the lucrative yacht charter and cruising business, but they were soon discovered by the local windsurfers. The possibility of having their own sail-maker with whom to work and experiment was enough to attract windsurfers from all over the island.

Rig development Up to now the local sailors had been using stock Windsurfers with bolted-on footstraps, and home-made daggerboards. They had been jumping waves, using standard sails on blue Windsurfer masts, that bent at the top as much as 30 in (76 cm) under a 20 lb (9 kg) load. It was very much like sailing with a rubber rig, and was totally unsatisfactory. There obviously had to be some radical re-designing, and Maui Sails set about it.

Their sail making experience had been gained through years of involvement in dinghy racing, and also hang-gliding. Indeed, many hang-gliders had, for some time, been bringing their more advanced wings in for repair. The evolution of the hang-glider wing was relatively far advanced, and had already come a long way from the original Delta profile. It had become much more wing-like, with anti-washout tips and high aspect profiles. Through watching the local windsurfers perform, Maui Sails came to the conclusion that shorter booms, higher clews, fatter shapes and more efficient profiles would promote a better jumping and flight performance.

Elliptical force The first problem was the top of the sail, which on a stock Windsurfer was pointed. Maui Sails soon spotted that the pointed top was crippling the efficiency of the sail. They diagnosed that the pointed sail had no elliptical force, and was generating a violent vortex that traveled down the leech of the sail, and interfered with the wind flowing across it. This meant that the sail could not generate lift, and instead a stall pattern was created along the upper portion of the sail. A more elliptical shape was needed if the sail was to function properly.

The way Maui Sails achieved this was to put an extension on the top of the sail, rather like the compression battens used in a dinghy sail. Furthermore, they told the windsurfers to cut 14 in (35.5 cm) off the top of their masts, and make up the height loss by putting extensions on the bottom, thus giving the masts a greater rigidity. The new sails were made from a good, heavy quality genoa-orientated 4½ oz (128 g) Dacron, and were a huge improvement in every respect.

The next development came in the foot of the sail. The standard Windsurfer sail had a rounded foot, which basically served as a kicking strap. As this was used to generate rig tension, the tightness of the foot

Sail Profiles

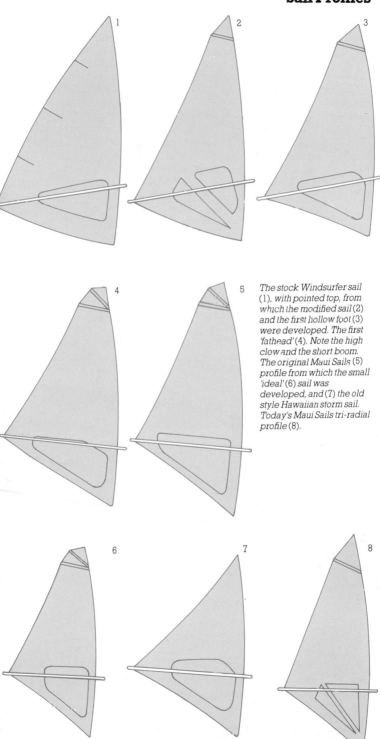

The stock Windsurfer sail (1), with pointed top, from which the modified sail (2) and the first hollow foot (3) were developed. The first 'fathead' (4). Note the high clow and the short boom. The original Maui Sails (5) profile from which the small 'ideal' (6) sail was developed, and (7) the old style Hawaiian storm sail. Today's Maui Sails tri-radial profile (8).

History of Funboard Sails

determined the tightness of the leech. However, it was not possible to tighten the rounded foot enough, and consequently it would wrinkle and flap in the wind, so Maui Sails decided to dispense with it altogether.

Sail development, once started, was incredibly quick, largely due to the perfect weather conditions of the Hawaiian islands. A sail could be tested in the morning, taken back for modifications, and then re-tested in the afternoon. The next change came with the introduction of a 'V'-shaped batten system, that was designed to maximize the functioning of the body of the sail. This was, however, later dropped in deference to a higher clew and shorter boom. The sail became known as a 'fathead', the others, of course, then became known as 'pinheads'.

Seams By now Maui Sails had developed a way of inserting the seam tapers so that the draft was held very far forward on the sail. It was an unusual way of drawing the seam tapers together, and other sail makers regarded it with some suspicion, but it worked well in holding the shape of the sail and made good use of the material. Having reached the desired sail profile and construction, there was now time for a few variations. A 40 ft^2 (3.7 m^2) sail was produced for use in 'ideal' Hawaiian conditions with a 12½ ft (3.8 m) mast, and a short, 6 ft (1.8 m) boom – the Hawaiian storm sail that is largely unchanged today. The success of all these developments in sail design has now been widely acknowledged by other sail manufacturers.

High aspect ratio Within the last year or so, the trend in sail design has been towards 'high aspect ratio' rigs. These have taller masts and shorter booms than usual. The raising of the foot and clew of the sail, combined with the shortening of the boom keeps the clew from catching in the wave face, and allows a greater freedom of movement in tight situations.

Betty Birrell (left top), *one of the first women to ride big waves, using an early Hawaiian storm sail. Ken Winner wave jumping with the old style of storm sail* (left bottom). *Notice the long standard boom. Maneuvers like the 'duck gybe'* (above) *have only become possible since the introduction of high clew sails and short booms. A modern high wind and surf sail* (right). *A 58 ft² (5.4 m²) tri-radial on a 6½ ft (2 m) boom from Maui Sails.*

Sail Materials

Dacron Also called Terylene, Dacron is made by spinning plastic fibers into a yarn. This is then woven into a fabric and heat treated. Until recently it was the most popular material for making sailcloth, and was extensively used for many types of sail.

However, with the advent of funboards and surf sailing, serious short-comings were discovered. Under the much greater stress the material experienced amid the breaking waves, it had a tendency to stretch, and permanently lose its shape.

Mylar A more recent development is Mylar. This is made from the same plastic, extruded into very thin sheets. It is considerably stronger and some 25% lighter than Dacron. Because of its multi-directional stability more and more sail-makers now prefer Mylar.

Originally the Mylar polyester film was laminated onto one side of the Dacron fiber cloth. Although this went some way toward strengthening the cloth, it remained unsatisfactory, as it was unbalanced and had different stretch characteristics on either side. In addition, it suffered from the main disadvantage of Dacron, namely that it absorbed water on that side, thereby increasing its weight. Mylar, on the other hand, does not absorb water, and is, to all intents and purposes, waterproof. It is without doubt, one of the best developments in sail manufacture.

Scrim laminate *Polyester scrim laminate is the latest development in sail material, and is marketed under several brand names, such as Duo Film. Polyester fibers are sandwiched between two layers of Mylar, giving a more stable and less brittle result than the previous one-sided lamination. It is also stronger and lighter, and has better shape retention characteristics.*

Material combinations
Some sails are made from material combinations, usually Dacron and Mylar. The luff panels can be made from Dacron to allow for some give in the curve, and to compensate for the bend characteristics of different masts. The rest is made from Mylar to make it strong and flat. The edge and top panels may be two-ply for extra strength.

Today a wide variety of shapes and cuts are in production (right), all enjoying varying degrees of popularity.

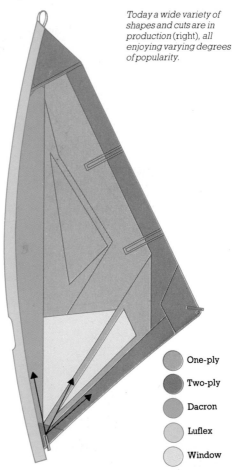

One-ply

Two-ply

Dacron

Luflex

Window

Radial cut *The panels are cut so that they radiate from the tack of the sail (right).*

Vertical cut sails Until the late 1970s, sails were always cross-cut with horizontal panels. Today the trend, and to some extent the fashion, is for vertical cut sails.

Once again, the main problem the sail makers had to overcome was how to construct a sail that would stand up to the punishment meted out by the surf sailors. The problem had traditionally revolved around the propensity of the seams to yield under stress and change the shape of the sail. By cutting the sail vertically this problem was overcome, while it had the added bonus of enabling the sail-maker to position the draft more accurately.

Before the advent of Mylar, it also made more sense to use the Dacron cloth vertically, as this was the direction in which it was manufactured. With the multi-directional stability of Mylar this is, of course, no longer a consideration. Since most of the tension radiates up and outwards from the tack of the sail, the vertical panels are also cut to radiate in this direction.

Sail design is a combination of fashion, cloth economy, and personal preference. The truth is, that a good sail designer can make a sail work in a variety of shapes and cuts. However, although research into sail profiles continues, it is now generally accepted that for high wind and surf sailing, the combination of vertical cut and Mylar produces a stronger sail.

Sail Types

Surf sails Assessing the size of sail required is dependent not only on wind strength, but also on the length of funboard it is to be used on. A long all round funboard can be used in light winds, and can take a sail of up to 86 ft² (8 m²). For a smaller funboard of around 10½ft (3.2 m), which would not normally be sailed in under a Force 4, a maximum sail size of between 60 ft² (5.5 m²) and 64 ft² (5.9 m²) should be adequate. If your board is a short sinker, and you only sail in a Force 5 and above, the largest sail you will need would be between 54 ft² (5 m²) and 60 ft² (5.5 m²). At the other extreme, for winds of around Force 8, a 38 ft² (3.5 m²) storm sail should suffice.

For surf sailing, always choose a sail that is as close as possible to the optimum size necessary for getting out through the surf and making good jumps. Since a wave riding board is so small, and the apparent wind generated when actually surfing is so great, it is easy to become overpowered, at which point you lose maneuverability.

A new generation, fully battened (left), high performance sail. Malte Simmer (below) with his famous and much copied scallop-edged sail, and (bottom) a Maui Sails tri-radial.

Racing sails Surf sails are not really suitable for racing on long boards. Even moderate surfing profile sails are not right for racing round courses. When using a long board with a high efficiency daggerboard, you need a sail with a greater chord length for powerful reaching, and for weather performance, a sail with a flatter shape that will give you the precise draft control you need.

By using a sliding mast track, the range of the racing sail is increased. In the forward position the nose of the board is forced down, allowing you to rake the mast aft and de-power. It also allows you to hang your weight on the rig more efficiently, so that you can handle a larger sail. A general indication of the racing sail size/wind strength relationship is: 70 ft^2 (6.6 m^2) for Force 4–5, (perhaps more for stronger sailors), 61 ft^2 (5.8 m^2) for Force 5–6, and 55 ft^2 (5.2 m^2) for anything stronger. For serious racing always aim to be slightly over-powered in the gusts, so that you have to luff the sail at times, to prevent yourself being pulled off the board.

Testing a prototype (below) of the new Stratos racing sail. (Right) A cross-cut, World Cup regatta sail, and (bottom) two World Cup racing sails at Torquay, Australia.

Booms, Masts, and Extensions

A few years ago, the average windsurfer would own a standard board and rig, and possibly a 'high performance' storm sail. The equipment potential was very low, with the only adjustment possible being a choice between two sails. Today the situation is very different, with most serious windsurfers having an array of high performance equipment and accessories. This would normally include a set of adjustable booms, ranging from 5½ ft (1.7 m) to 8 ft (2.4 m), mast extensions of up to 16 in (40.5 cm), and a stiff and durable mast.

Booms To hold the required leech tension, it is important that the clew grommet be positioned not more than 2 in (5 cm) from the boom end. Due to the large range of sail sizes now available it has, therefore, become necessary to have adjustable booms. There are today two types on the market – telescopic and add-on. The advantage of a telescopic adjustable boom is that you do not have to carry around a number of individual extensions that invariably get lost. The disadvantage is that, unless lubricated regularly, the salt water quickly corrodes the internal section and locks it up. The opposite considerations apply to the add-on type.

Most adjustable booms have innertube flaps to keep the water out, but these often peel back during wipe-outs. Another problem is the damage caused when sand gets into the telescoping part. Always rinse your

The add-on type adjustable boom (top). Note the range of extension pieces. Extending a telescopic adjustable boom (above).

To build up the tension required for setting a high performance rig, an outhaul pulley system is used. It may provide a double or triple purchase.

Development in sail design is moving towards shorter and shorter booms, like this 44 in (112 cm) prototype. They are a great advantage when wave sailing.

booms after use, and use Vaseline to lubricate all moving parts.

The ideal boom end is one that is compact and that can easily be secured, tightly, to the mast. The rear end should have two or three rollers, to permit a double or triple outhaul purchase. The boom itself should be as stiff as possible, and should preferably be made of 60/61 tensile aluminum. Two diameters are currently available, 1¼ in (3 cm) and 1⅜ in (3.5 cm), to cater for windsurfers with small and large hands.

The standard grip for production boards is made from vulcanized rubber coating, which, although very durable, can cause soft hands to blister. Alternatively, most custom board sailors use a spongy, ¹⁄₁₆ in (1.6 mm) thick, grip that is glued to the boom with Neoprene Cement. It is much softer on the hands but is liable to wear out.

Masts Always match your mast to the type of sailing you intend to do. For racing use a very stiff mast, preferably made of aluminum, and for wave sailing use a stiff *and* durable mast made from a fiberglass/epoxy combination. Both mast constructions have individual performance characteristics that suit the type of sailing they are designed for. Aluminum combines a great rigidity with strength, and will therefore help the sail keep its shape. However, it is vulnerable to sudden stress and will kink, and is therefore not suitable for wave sailing. Fiberglass, on the other hand, will flex under a sudden load, and, while this will decrease sail efficiency, it *will* stay in one piece. Carbon fiber is stiff, but is similar to aluminum in that it will fail under a sudden load, and is not suitable for wave sailing.

Mast base extensions With so many different sail sizes now on the market, all with different mast sock lengths, it has become necessary to use a mast base extension to keep the tack of the sail a constant distance from the deck. There are two types of extension now commonly in use, the add-on type which consists of an adaptor and extension pieces, and the long extension with adjustable collet type. Both have their problems. The first suffers from a vulnerability to sand jamming, while the second has strength deficiencies, due to the series of adjustment holes. Always remember that the mast base must fit tightly into the mast, as a loose fit will set up uneven stresses that can split it. It is often a good idea to reinforce a fiberglass mast, as even with a tight fit it may split.

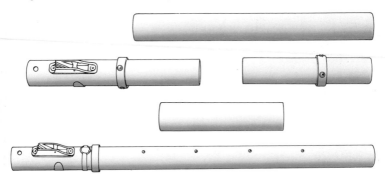

The two types of mast base extension (above), add-on and adjustable. The downhaul pulley system (right) is a must for high performance rig setting.

Setting a High Performance Rig

Setting a high performance rig well is the key to windsurfing success and enjoyment. It is a highly sensitive piece of equipment that will respond to delicate adjustment and tuning more than an ordinary rig. It is in many ways the most crucial factor in a board's performance.

Rig efficiency accounts for at least 50% of your total equipment potential, and unless your sail is set properly you will not be able to exploit the full capability of your board. While many of the procedures involved are the same as those for setting an ordinary rig, a high performance rig requires more sensitive treatment.

One of the main points to bear in mind, is that the modern high wind sail requires extreme downhaul and outhaul tensioning for it to achieve its correct shape. To this end a pulley system is necessary. If possible, choose one which gives you a triple purchase.

Use whatever base extensions are necessary to make the tack of the sail 8–14 in (20–35 cm) from the universal joint. Pad out any slackness in the extension collar with pattern Mylar or tape.

Slide the mast into the sail sleeve, and attach the mast foot to the board. Lightly tension the downhaul in preparation for inserting the battens.

An effective way to ensure that your boom is attached tightly, is to align it, on the ground, parallel with the mast.

To attach the boom, make a knot and a noose. Pass the noose down through the uphaul hole and back round the mast, so that the noose fits over the knot.

Swing the boom down at right angles to the mast, so that the knot locks it tight. Do not do this with a cheap mast, as it is liable to split under the tension.

Tension the outhaul nearly to the limit. Use a thin cord so that you can pass it through the clew eye at least twice to aid tensioning. If necessary use your foot.

Alternatively, use a pulley system. For really serious windsurfers this is indispensable, as it is the only way to get maximum rig tension.

Re-tension the downhaul, this time to the limit. Again, use your foot and a pulley system if necessary.

Check the tension of the outhaul, and if satisfactory insert the head battens.

Remember to use a mast pad to protect your board. Without a pad the board will very quickly suffer structural damage.

Finally set the sail in the wind on the beach. Make sure it looks and feels right, and if necessary make adjustments.

Sail Faultfinding

While most mass-produced sails will function quite adequately with the minimum attention, a modern high performance sail requires delicate tuning and setting if its potential is to be realized. Far too many windsurfers fail to pay adequate attention to this critical factor in board performance, and consequently never fully exploit their equipment's capability, or their own technique. Furthermore, a badly set sail is more likely to stretch, or even tear.

Getting enough rig tension is vital, and if you do not have one of the pulley systems currently available, then improvise. For the downhaul and outhaul use a strong thin line passed through the eyelets several times. This will effectively give you a double or triple purchase, and will make the extreme tensioning required for high performance sail setting much easier.

Not enough downhaul
(left) *Note the horizontal wrinkles. Tighten downhaul. Check tension after 20 minutes sailing.*

Not enough outhaul (right)
Note baggy sail shape. This will shift the CE back in gusts, and make the sail unmanageable. Tighten outhaul and re-test.

Too much downhaul (left)
The luff is too flat, and the mast is excessively bent. Slacken downhaul until desired shape is achieved.

Too much outhaul (right)
Sail is completely flat, and will lack power. Slacken outhaul until correct draft is obtained in the luff area.

No batten tension (left)
Wrinkles running vertically to the batten. Increase tension until they disappear.

Battens too flexible (right)
Battens are bent. Replace with stiffer battens, preferably tapered.

Too much batten tension
(left) *Batten assumes 'S' shape. Reduce tension.*

Blown or stretched sail (right) *Sail is unmanageable in gusts, and is impossible to set without a full head or flat foot.*

Sail Care and Folding

Perfectly set sail After all adjustments have been made, set the sail in the wind. Check to see that there are no wrinkles, or loose lines, and make sure that the boom is tight against the mast. A few extra minutes spent checking the rig, could mean less time spent trying to make adjustments with cold hands.

Sail care and folding All sails need to be looked after properly, especially those made of Mylar. Although slightly more expensive than others, a Mylar sail, if treated correctly, will last a long time. Be very careful when handling your sails to watch out for any sharp objects – they can ruin a sail in seconds.

If there are no facilities at the beach for you to wash and dry your sail, there is nothing wrong with removing the battens and rolling it up around the mast, as long as you loosen off the downhaul first. If you intend to carry it on the top of a car, always put it in a mast/sail bag, as a flapping sail will damage itself.

Whenever possible, you should follow this procedure at the end of a day's sailing. (1) Wash the sail in fresh water. (2) Let it dry on the mast. (3) Take it off the mast and roll it up from head to foot, leaving the battens in. (4) Store it rolled up in a lightproof bag, and lay it down flat. This procedure does not take long, and will increase your sail's life expectancy.

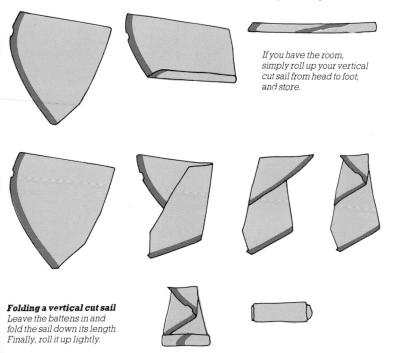

If you have the room, simply roll up your vertical cut sail from head to foot, and store.

Folding a vertical cut sail
Leave the battens in and fold the sail down its length. Finally, roll it up lightly.

Choosing a Funboard Sail

Choosing the right sail used to be straightforward. Most boards were supplied with a large regatta sail, to which people would add a storm sail for high winds. Unfortunately they tended to try and cut costs on this second sail, and buy a not very strong one, when in fact it usually got the hardest treatment. Today the situation is very different, with an apparently endless array of vertical and cross-cuts, Dacron and Mylar, pinheads, plumpheads, and fatheads available.

Your local windsurfing shop will undoubtedly have a huge selection of sails that will not make your choice any easier. However, this does mean that most large manufacturers will be represented. As a rule, it is better to buy one of their sails, for the simple reason that it will have been tried and tested in the toughest conditions before being marketed to the public. On these grounds, it is probably not advisable to buy from a small sail-maker, who may not have the necessary testing facilities. In addition, it should be said that the quality of most production sails is now very high, as a result of the latest computerized cutting and stitching equipment.

Always buy the best sail you can afford and look after it – a good sail will last a long time. If you can buy a Mylar vertical cut sail, do – they are quite simply the best! Most reputable manufacturers now produce them, so ask around and compare reports before deciding on which brand.

Sail compatibility When buying a new sail, it is important to ensure that it is compatible with the equipment you already have. For example, is it compatible with the rigidity characteristics of your mast? Will you need a mast extension? And, what size boom will you require?

A good selection of sails you might choose would be a 58 ft² (5.4 m²), a 50 ft² (4.6 m²), and a 38 ft² (3.5 m²). All three are designed to fit a stiff surf mast, and the different luff heights are catered for by extending the luff socks on the smaller sails. Alternatively, you may prefer to use two different masts, or a two-piece mast with different top sizes. The first two sails take a 6½ ft (2 m) boom, the last a 5½ ft (1.7 m) boom.

58 ft² (5.4 m²) *One of the most widely used sizes. Suitable for light to moderate conditions.*

50 ft² (4.6 m²) *A good mid-range size, for use in 'lively' conditions.*

38 ft² (3.5 m²) *For use in extreme conditions. Note the length of the luff sock.*

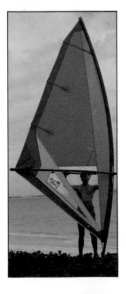

Sail checklist Points to look for when buying a new sail.

Make sure there is heavy reinforcement of the top of the mast sleeve, to protect it from dragging and scuffing.

Batten pockets should also be heavily reinforced.

Try to avoid sails with a lot of stitching near the edges – it can come apart, and weakens the material.

The wishbone cut-out, a high stress area, should have reinforcement to protect against wear.

The tack of the sail should be reinforced, and have heavy duty eyelets to take the strain of rig tensioning.

The foot of the sail can be damaged by being dragged across the footstraps and the non-slip deck, and must be reinforced.

The clew must be reinforced, and have heavy duty eyelets. Static rig tension can be as much as 180 lbs (81.5 kg).

The Wing

Without doubt the most exciting development in today's rig technology has been the arrival of the 'Wing'. Within six months of its introduction into windsurfing, it was used to smash the world speed record, clocking a speed of 30.82 knots.

The Wing is a revolutionary new way of replacing the traditional flexible mast enclosed in a luff sleeve. The problem with the conventional mast/sail link-up, was that a wind shadow area was formed behind the mast on the leeward side of the sail, which created turbulence. The foil-shaped Wing mast on the other hand, has a slot in the trailing edge into which the sail fits, allowing the leeward curve of the mast to flow smoothly into the leeward curve of the sail. The Wing mast also presents a perfect foil to the wind, unlike the clumsy, rounded, leading edge of the traditional mast, and thus creates far less drag.

Rigidity Unlike a conventional spar, the Wing is almost completely rigid, with no flex fore or aft. This means that in high winds and gusts the mast does not flex. When a conventional spar flexes, there is a tendency for the draft, or camber, of the sail to shift backward. This usually results in the sailor losing control. With the Wing, the draught does not move, and so in gusts the board accelerates, rather than the sailor becoming overpowered. This point has certainly been proved in speed trials, where sailors using conventional spars have come up against a 27-28 knots barrier.

This rigidity in the Wing allows the use of full-length battens, which enable the rider to control the sail's shape to a greater degree. It also makes possible the attachment of a trapeze line about half-way up the Wing, which then connects onto the regular harness lines, giving the rider a more efficient leverage.

Production The production method used to achieve this degree of rigidity in the Wing, is similar to that used in the production of container ships, Admiral's Cup racing yachts, and space shuttle doors! Carbon fiber is pre-impregnated with a heat sensitive catalyst, and then laid up. It is then vacuum pressed together, and baked in an oven. The oven builds slowly up to a certain temperature, holds it for a while, and then slowly cools down. This 'curing' process is used to achieve a perfect resin to fabric mix, which gives the maximum strength to weight ratio.

At about $9\frac{1}{2}$ lbs (4.3 kg), the Wing weighs nearly 3 lbs (1.4 kg) more than an average surf mast, not taking into account the extra weight of a wet conventional mast sleeve. In return for this small amount of extra weight it does, however, have roughly an extra 11 ft^2 (1m^2) of surface area, which adds to the lift potential of the whole rig.

Sail control The Wing further differs from a conventional mast in that it has four sail controls, the downhaul, the outhaul, the kicking strap, and the rotation of the mast. This last control is the most important, and enables the sailor to select, for example, a narrow angle of attack with a flat foil shape, which has the draft further back, or a wide angle of attack with a deep foil shape, which positions the draft further forward.

The actual increase in rig efficiency made possible by the Wing has yet to be fully determined, but early estimates indicate that it is something in the region of 15–20%· Development is already under way to produce a 'wing' for surf sailing. If successful, it will probably result in surf rig sail areas of between 25–45 ft^2 (2.3-4.2 m^2) being used.

In terms of recreational sailing, the greater rig efficiency the Wing makes possible will lower the planing barrier. Sailing a funboard will then be feasible in much lighter winds, as the board will be quicker to plane, and the smaller rig easier to handle.

Barry Spanier of Maui Sails (above), Hawaii checking out a prototype Wing sail. Dimitrije Milovich (above right) of Weathersports, Salt Lake City, the inventor of the Wing.

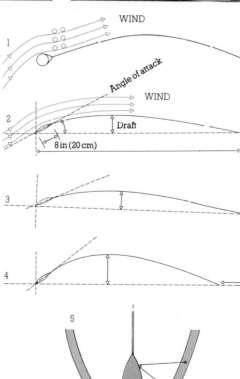

A conventional mast and mast sleeve (1), has a wind shadow that creates turbulence. This lowers rig efficiency. The Wing (2), on the other hand, has no wind shadow. It presents a perfect foil to the wind, and promotes a smooth and uninterrupted airflow. The angle of attack determines the draft's position. A narrow angle (3) positions the draft further back, than a wide angle (4). The Wing's boom (5) is wider than usual, to allow the 8 in (12.7 cm) spar to rotate through 45° either side of the center. This is done by a system of pulleys and cleats.

Funboard Techniques

*The short board has been the most exciting development in the history of windsurfing. To have fun **and** survive in high winds and surf, requires not only the right equipment, but also a good technique. Learn to master rapid water starts and fast fluid gybes, and you will very quickly find out why they are called funboards!*

Carrying the Board and Rig

There is nothing more embarrassing than to pick up your board and rig, and walk confidently down the beach, only to have the wind whip the sail through 360° and dump you and the board in the sand! Sooner or later it happens to everybody. However, it *is* possible to carry the board and rig to the water quite safely even in the windiest conditions, if the following considerations are borne in mind. Always stand to windward of the board and rig. Always keep the front of the boom and the luff of the sail pointing into the wind. Practice carrying a short board and a long board – they need different techniques. Practice your launching, so that as soon as you reach the water you can get sailing. This technique is not difficult, and will save you and your equipment from unnecessary wear and tear.

Making it look easy! Just support the mast with one hand (right), and hold a footstrap with the other. Alternatively, support the sail on your head (left).

On really windy days things can get out of hand. Always point the luff of the sail into the wind (below), or you may part company with it.

A convenient method of carrying a short board is to put it on top of the sail (left), especially if you have a long walk.

The Short Board Launch

Stand to windward of the board (1), and hold the mast just below the boom end with your front hand. Take hold of one of the front footstraps with your rear hand, lift up the board and balance the sail on your head. Walk down to the water with the sail luffing (2) and go in knee-deep. Lower the board into the water (3), pushing the mast forward to keep the board pointing across the wind. Take hold of the boom and step toward the board, consciously pushing the rig forward (4). Step onto the board with your back foot (5), sheet in, and then step on with your front foot and start sailing (6).

Remember to always keep upwind of the board, and that it needs to be at least 110° off the wind for launching.

The Long Board Launch

Stand to windward of the board, and position the hull across the wind (1). Hold the boom as before and lift the board's tail with your back hand (2). Slide the board down the beach (3) and enter the water (4) (5). Release the tail and transfer both hands to the boom (6), all the time pushing the rig toward the nose of the board. It may be necessary to walk toward the board to keep it from heading up. Step onto the board with your back foot first (7), sheet in, and then step on with your front foot (8) and start sailing.

Sometimes when entering the water, the

nose may bury itself in the first wave. If this happens, release the tail and push the rig toward the nose to stop the board heading up.

Harnesses

The harness is now an integral part of windsurfing equipment. It consists of a hook attached to the sailor's chest, and a rope loop on the boom, and is designed to take the strain off the sailor's arms. Medical evidence suggests that long-term sailing without the aid of a harness, can put undue stresses on the ligaments in both the wrists and elbows, and can lead to elongation, so wear one!

Harness lines Usually made of ¼ in (6.4 mm) diameter Dacron line, they are attached to the boom with straps, which protect the boom grip from wearing. The harness hook is attached by simply swinging the line towards the body. The positioning of the straps is critical, and requires patient adjustment. They are usually positioned between the normal hand positions, with at the maximum, an 18 in (45.5 cm) loop. The straps *must* be the same distance from each hand, or one will bear the greater strain, and will tire quickly.

The harness There are basically two types of sailboard harness – the conventional single hook, and the spreader.

The single hook harness has been around for eight years, and is now considered obsolete by most experienced sailors. Its main drawback was found to be the webbing under the hook's plate, which under tension tended to constrict the ribs and cause bruising.

The spreader harness avoids this problem by transferring the webbing tension onto the wearer's back, where it can be borne more easily. The hook is fixed to a stainless steel or plastic spreader bar, and has two attachment points to prevent rope wear and tangling.

Harness technique The sooner you learn to use a harness, the sooner you will be able to stay out on the water for long periods of time. However, if you are still having catapult falls in strong winds, then wait a while, as catapulting in a harness can be dangerous!

To hook in, swing the line towards your body and engage the hook with a downwards motion of the torso. To unhook, simply slacken the line tension by pulling the boom towards you, and the line will drop out. Practice this on the land first, and then try it out on the water. Once hooked in keep a look out for gusts and be ready to sheet out.

Hanging your weight on the harness (right) leaves your arms free to control the boom, while your feet control the board.

Thin gauge plastic tubing (above) is used to prevent the line wearing out. The spreader harness (right). Note the 'V'-shaped hook, which stops the line tangling.

Water Starts

Three years ago the water start was considered as solely a free-style trick, and not a practicable way of mounting the board. Today, however, it is regarded as normal practice, especially for boards under 9 ft (2.7 m).

Although quite a tricky maneuver, it does not take long to master, provided the conditions are right. Once perfected, it is much easier than uphauling, and far less tiring.

For wave sailing the water start is crucial. The ability to quickly restart after a wipe-out is the key to protecting your equipment in surf conditions. An experienced wave sailor should be able to water start after a jump landing in under a second, failure to do so could result in the sailor and board getting a severe pounding from a breaking wave.

Equipment preparation
Your mast must be sealed, and the boom no more than chin high. The board should be a floater or semi-floater to begin with. Only move on to a sinker when you have mastered the technique. If possible use a high aspect ratio, short boom sail for greater leverage.

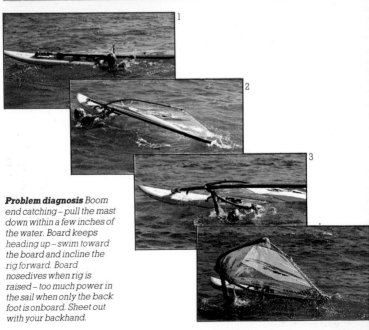

Problem diagnosis Boom end catching – pull the mast down within a few inches of the water. Board keeps heading up – swim toward the board and incline the rig forward. Board nosedives when rig is raised – too much power in the sail when only the back foot is onboard. Sheet out with your backhand.

The mast must be at right angles to the wind so as to expose the maximum luff area, so you must swim it into position (1). Hold the mast with your front hand, and while treading water push it up until the boom clears the water (2). If the boom back end drags and does not clear, push the mast down a little until the wind pressure clears it. When the sail clears the water, transfer your hands to the boom (3) and, keeping the sail as high as possible, swim toward the board (4). To help head the board off the wind push the mast toward the nose (5). Swimming toward the board will also help this. Place your back foot on the tail of the board (6) while still treading water with your front foot. This will provide extra lift and will stop the board drifting off the wind. When the board is about 120° off the wind kick hard with your front foot (7), and if the wind is light pump the sail. Raise yourself onto the board (8) keeping the back leg bent to lower the center of gravity. Hold your arms high to keep the rig upright and expose the maximum sail area. With the board beginning to move (9) get your front foot on and start sailing (10).

Carved Gybe

The original method of gybing on longer boards, called the 'flare gybe', consisted of stalling the board by standing on the tail and making the turn by manipulating the rig. The board did turn, but only at the cost of a total loss of speed. Carved gybes were first introduced on the Windsurfer Rocket boards, and consisted of a wide turn on the inside rail. With the advent of shorter and shorter boards, the carved gybe became more widely practiced, as it is very difficult to tack a short board.

The radius and speed of the gybe are determined by the hull design of the board used. A suitable board for learning would be one with enough buoyancy when stationary to support the sailor, but need not necessarily be uphaulable. The buoyancy is needed to give 'follow through' to the turns. Tail width should be about 12–16 in (35–40 cm), and the skeg arrangement should be able to handle speed work without spinning out. Rig efficiency is also important. If possible use a high aspect ratio, short boom sail, but make sure you are not over-powered. The key to learning to carve gybes quickly and efficiently, is a total commitment to the move. Any holding back will result in a wipe-out

Carved Gybe

The approach The speed
of the approach is very
important (1), and takes
practice to gauge. If you are
under-powered, pump the
sail and try to reach planing
speed. If you are
over-powered you must
sheet out and slow down.
(2) Remove your back foot
from its footstrap, place it
near the inside rail, push
down, and start pulling up
with your front foot in its
footstrap. The board will
begin to turn so you must
trim the sail by tilting the
rig back a little. With the
board turning on the inside
rail (3), lean into the turn,
pulling up with your front
foot and pushing down with
your back foot. Now move
your front hand close to the
boom end (4), release your
back hand, and let the sail
flip. Going through the
downwind position is the
'make or break' point of the
gybe. You must be positive
and continue leaning or the
turn will fail. Having passed
through the eye of the wind
(5) pivot the sail on your
front hand, and move your
back hand to the mast. Shift
your weight onto the front
foot a little, so as to flatten
the board while still
digging the tail in. Continue

leaning and carving with your feet (6) while changing hand positions so that they are reversed. Begin to sheet in while transferring your weight forward. Finish the gybe (7) by switching your feet positions and transfer your front hand from the mast to the boom. A successful carved gybe completed (8).

Duck Gybe

The duck gybe was 'invented' by the Hawaiian windsurfer, Richard Whyte, in the summer of 1981. At the time it was dismissed as a bit of a pointless trick, and was considered to be of no real use. However, by the spring of the following year the duck gybe had spread throughout the Hawaiian Islands, and had been mastered by all the top sailors. It was no longer a clumsy and jerky boom-to-sail-to-boom trick, but a polished and smooth boom-to-boom transition. The duck gybe took these early pioneers nearly nine months to perfect, but a competent short board sailor today should be able to do it in a week of good winds.

The ideal board for the duck gybe is a semi-sinker with a wide point forward of center, equipped with a high aspect ratio rig with the foot of the sail as far off the deck as possible.

Finally, bear in mind that the motions involved in a duck gybe are identical in nearly every respect to those used for a carved gybe, the main difference being that the rig is flipped overhead.

Duck Gybe

Approach the gybe on a plane (1), at about the same speed as for a conventional gybe. Begin to carve the board round (2), concentrating on keeping the right speed. As you approach the dead downwind position, release your front hand and take hold of the boom behind your back hand (3). Remember to lean into the turn and keep the board carving round. Now release your back hand from the boom and in one motion (with your old front hand) throw the sail overhead and duck (4). Reach with your old back hand under the sail and take hold of the front of the boom, while continuing to carve the turn. With both hands on the boom on the new tack (5), slide them into the proper positions, and begin to tilt the rig back. Be careful to sheet out a little, and continue to carve the board round. With the board almost completely turned, shift your weight forward a bit to flatten it, and continue planing. Begin switching feet positions (6), moving the back foot forward first.

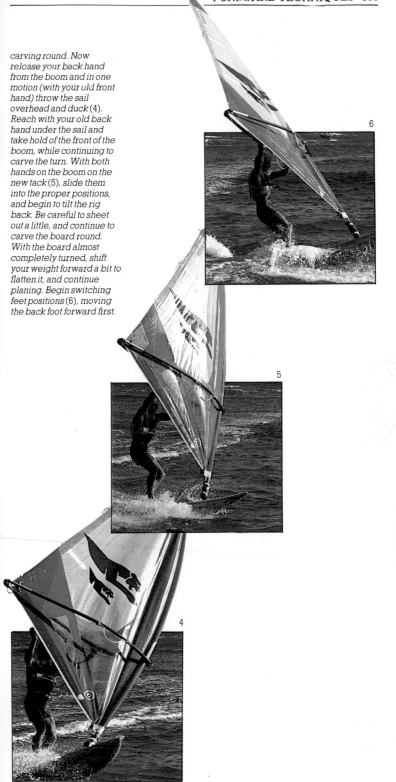

One-Handed Gybe

The one-handed gybe is really just a free-style trick, and is regarded by most people as a piece of showmanship. As a turning maneuver it is of limited use, and it is very difficult to complete a one-handed gybe as smoothly as a regular gybe. There are two types of one-handed gybe, the conventional and the duck, both of which are variations of other gybes. The one-handed conventional gybe is identical to the conventional gybe in almost every respect, the only difference being that when the back hand is released from the boom it is dragged in the water, (below).

It is advisable to practice this maneuver away from other windsurfers, and out of sight of any spectators on the beach. It is a difficult technique to master and involves a lot of falling in, so if you want to look good, learn it first!

One-Handed Duck Gybe

In almost every respect, the steps involved are identical to those used for a standard duck gybe. The variation comes with the hand drag.

Approach the gybe as you would for a two-handed duck gybe (1). Begin to carve the turn (2), while at the same time transferring your front hand to a position behind your back hand on the boom. This will make the rig fall away from the wind. Continue to carve the turn, release your back hand and simultaneously throw the sail (3) over your head with your front hand, and drag your back hand in the water for a few seconds. Take hold of the front of the boom on the new tack with this hand, and complete the duck gybe as usual (4).

Problems Sail control is lost as soon as the back hand is dragged in the water – keep the center of gravity low, and try to flip the sail over in as upright a position as possible. Always remember to keep carving the turn all the way through the gybe.

Surf Sailing

Sailing in surf can be dangerous, and should only be attempted by a competent windsurfer who is fully aware of the risks involved. Before entering the water, potential surf sailors must be confident that both their equipment and their technique are up to it.

Equipment Always use equipment that is suitable for the conditions and your level of windsurfing experience. Make sure that you are familiar with the board and rig you intend to use – riding a wave is no time to discover that your board is not buoyant enough. Likewise, do not try to learn to sail a sinker in surf conditions. If your board has a sharp nose you must round it off (or have it done professionally), and do the same to the tip and trailing edge of the fins. A sharp nose or fin can be dangerous in a wipe-out, and could even be fatal!

Always check all your gear thoroughly before going sailing. Keep a special look out for frayed ropes, loose skegs, grommets working their way out, and power joint wear. An equipment failure at sea could cost you your life. Modern harnesses have a backpack, so make use of it and carry a spare line, fin, and flare.

Wind Never sail in an offshore wind. Equipment failures do happen, and if you are beyond the wave breakline an offshore wind will make it almost impossible to get back in. Look out for changes in wind direction – what was a cross offshore when you started sailing could change while you are out on the water.

Currents Always ask about local currents before going sailing. If you get caught in one, swim across it, never against it.

The sea floor Try to keep your feet off the sea floor at all times, even if it is sandy. Getting a foot full of sea-urchin spines or a severe cut from a coral reef can be very painful, and tends to take a long time to heal. If you do get cut in tropical conditions, it is very important to clean out any sand particles after sailing with a soft toothbrush.

Lifeguards and locals When sailing at a new location ask the locals about the prevalent conditions, and have a chat with the lifeguards. Be nice to them because if you get into trouble they will be the people coming to rescue you! Always behave yourself and obey any local rules, or you may alienate the locals and give the sport a bad name.

Wetsuits If you need to wear a wetsuit, make sure it is a good fit. You must be able to swim in it, so a baggy or overly tight suit is no good. In extreme conditions it is generally a bad idea to wear a full drysuit. It could fill with water and make swimming almost impossible.

Safety in the surf is really a question of having the right attitude and being sensible. Never take unnecessary risks, whether it be with your equipment, your technique, or with other people. Always sail with a friend so that you can keep an eye on each other, and always be prepared for any eventuality. Lastly, watch out for surfers. They were on the waves first, and you should always give way to them.

Wipe-outs *Allan Cadiz (left) having a wipe-out after just making it over a wave in an offshore wind.*

Bottom turns *Mis-timing the bottom turn (right) can cause a collision with the lip, and a risk of the boom hitting you in the face.*

Rocks and currents *A typical rocky headland (below). Watch out for currents and submerged rocks, and be very careful when sailing past not to get caught out by a set wave.*

Wave Sailing

Wave sailing is the most spectacular and exhilarating aspect of windsurfing, and indeed of all water sports. The combination of wind and waves presents a unique challenge to the windsurfer, a challenge few can resist. Over the last three years, with the advent of the short 'sinker' boards, the scope of wave riding and jumping techniques has been revolutionized. Contrary to popular belief, wave sailing is not as hard as it looks, and, given a good basic technique it should be within most people's reach.

Wave Riding

On a short sailboard, the movements made in riding a wave are very similar to those used on a conventional surf-board. In fact, wave riding on a sailboard is considerably easier than on a surf-board, as the former can generate its own speed independent of the waves, whereas the latter can not. In surfing, the rider has to be in the right place at the right time, and must start paddling at exactly the right moment to catch the wave, (usually when it is critical). Once up and riding, there is a limit to the amount of speed that can be generated by 'pumping' the board. This means that if a section of the wave collapses it is very difficult to get round it. On a sailboard, it is possible to catch a wave out to sea before it gets critical, and also to 'power' round any collapsed sections. In addition, the sailboard rider can counteract excessive leaning in turns and near falls by simply sheeting in the sail.

Roller coaster rides Once on a wave, it is possible to make carving turns up and down the face of the wave, dropping down and making a hard turn, projecting back up to the top and making another hard turn back down to the bottom to repeat the whole process again. The free-falling, high-speed sensation this creates is difficult to describe in words, suffice it to say that once experienced it is addictive.

Courage The level of competence you achieve in wave riding will largely be determined by how courageous and confident you are. Sailing in big waves is not difficult, but it can be if you lack the courage to risk a wipe-out, or if you are not confident that you will be able to hold your breath for long enough.

Robby Naish (left bottom) executing a critical 'off-the-lip' turn. Note how the wave is closing out toward him. Richard Whyte (right) riding backside dead into the wind, with the sail nearly luffing. An 'off-the-lip re-entry' (below). Note how the sail is supporting the rider, as he uses his front foot to bring the board back round, while his back foot is pushing from left to right. 'Dropping into' a big Diamond Head wave (bottom) in an offshore wind. The wave is closing out, and is only ridable in a straight line toward the beach.

Wave Riding

*Making a bottom turn (below).
Note how the boom end is
almost catching in the
wave. Performing a top turn
(right top) on a small wave,
in a cross, onshore, wind.
Note the track of the board,
from left to right on the
wave. Using the crest of the
wave to redirect the board
in a top turn. (right middle).
The rider is about to
depress the tail with his
back foot, to point the
board back down the
wave. Mike Fairchild (right
bottom) 'cutting back' on a
wave at Diamond Head,
Hawaii. Note how only the
tip of the tail is acutally on
the wave.*

Gybing on Waves

Just as it is easier to turn a car at speed on a banked rather than flat corner, it is easier to gybe on a wave than on a flat or choppy surface. Gybing on a wave allows the rider to maintain a greater speed throughout the turn, and thus makes it easier to stay on a plane. It also greatly reduces the risk of a 'spin-out'. The only difficulties with this maneuver are timing the start of the turn and judging the speed of the wave. The ideal conditions for gybing on a wave are a Force 4-5 wind, in any direction except dead onshore or offshore, and 2-4 ft (.6-1.2 m) waves, preferably not 'hollow' or heavy shore breakers. Use the same equipment as that for the conventional and duck gybes.

The gybe Approach the wave on a plane. The wave must not be critical, and you should aim to complete the gybe before it breaks.

Begin carving the turn before you reach the base of the wave, and as the nose of the board rises up the wave face, release your back hand and continue carving the turn. (Ideally the sail should flip as the board reaches the high point of the wave.) When the board hits the high point, place your back hand on the mast to pivot the sail, and continue to carve the turn around and down the face. At the bottom of the wave, place your new back hand on the boom, sheet in, take hold with your new front hand and continue sailing. Timing is of the utmost importance when gybing on a wave, and it is not easy to get it right immediately. Be really positive, holding back will only result in failing to make the move. Concentrate on the foot and hand movements, but do not forget to check before attempting the move that there is not another sailor overtaking you downwind who you might collide with. Also, keep an eye on the speed of the wave, or you may find it overtaking *you*!

The key to a successful wave gybe is the early release of the back hand, and a reliance on the speed of the board and the speed of the wave to complete the turn. The combination of all these factors will result in a smooth and fast turn.

Problems A common problem people experience with this gybe, is continually sailing out of the back of the wave. This comes about through bad timing, and can be avoided by beginning to carve the turn earlier. If you are finding it difficult to control the board when the sail flips, try leaning further back as you come out of the turn at the bottom of the wave, and concentrate on pivoting the rig round your mast hand. And lastly, if you are completely slowing down at the high point of the wave, try to create extra speed up the face and shift your weight forward a little to flatten the board and keep it planing.

'Off-the-lip' When gybing off the lip of a small wave (right), it is important for the lip to hit the underside of the board. With the wind across the wave the sail will flip on contact. **Gybing on a wave** Note the track of the board (left bottom), and the way the sail is flipping as the board passes through the downwind position. At this point body-weight must be shifted back to allow for the steepness of the drop back down the wave.

'Off-the-lip' gybes Gybing off-the-lip, or critical, section of the wave demands an extra degree of wave experience, confidence, and determination. It should not be attempted by the inexperienced, or by the faint-hearted.

Choose a small wave that is about to break, and time the gybe so that as the sail flips the underside of the hull meets the falling lip. As the board rises up the face release your back hand and take hold of the mast. With the sail luffing and about to flip, use the speed of the board to carve up to the lip. As the underside hits the lip, (and the sail flips across the nose), shift your weight to the tail in anticipation of the drop. When you reach the base of the wave, sheet in and sail away.

Problems Sometimes when the board hits the lip it is spun around through a 250° turn. To counteract this tendency try to carve more on the inside rail, and this will straighten the board up. If you find the board nosediving as it reaches the base of the wave, remember to shift your weight back to the tail before the drop.

Gybing in the chop One of the many problems with gybing in choppy water is that the board tends to take off from the wavelets while going through the turn, causing a spin or 'slide-out'. To avoid this try to find a wavelet – no matter how small – to bank off. It will make control during the turn much easier, and will help the board stay on a plane.

Duck gybing on waves Approach the wave on a plane. Begin carving the turn before you reach the base of the wave, and as the nose rises up the wave face start the standard duck gybe procedure. Remember that both hands must be on the boom on the new tack as the board drops back down the face.

Problems To begin with, performing a duck gybe on a wave is a bit tricky, and a mistake often made is to let the sail get stuck halfway through the 'flip', resulting in the board going out through the back of the wave. This is largely due to a lack of commitment in carving the turn up the face and back off the top of the wave. Really concentrate on 'slashing' with your back foot at the high point. The other major problem with this gybe is that the sail becomes over-powered, and gets out of control while being flipped. This usually happens when there is a side, offshore wind. The apparent wind combines with the true wind, to make the wind experienced when dropping back into the wave much greater. To gybe in these conditions, use a slightly smaller sail and 'pump' it to gain speed before meeting the wave.

Top Turns/Off-the-Lip Turns

'Off-the-lip' and 'top' turns are, after wave jumping, the most spectacular moves in surf sailing. They demand the highest degree of skill, judgment, and timing, and take even the most experienced windsurfers a long time to master. Wipe-outs are a frequent occurrence, and bring with them the risk of equipment damage and personal injury. The difference between the two turns is that the 'off-the-lip' is executed in the critical section of the wave peak, while the 'top' is executed in the peak of the wave but not in the critical section.

Top Turns/Off-the-Lip Turns

Top turns (left) Project the board up the wave face to a section of the wave that is not critical. Just before you reach the peak, put intense pressure on the heel of your back foot and shift all your weight back, tilt the rig back and keep it sheeted in. The board will now make a tight 140° turn. When it faces back down the wave, trim the sail and lean forward to reduce the pressure on your back foot. As you reach the base of the wave lean back a little to stop the board nosediving, and get ready for the bottom turn.

Points to note are the back foot depressing the rear inside rail, in conjunction with the front foot pulling the board around.

Problems If the tail slides out during the turn, push harder with your back heel.

Off-the-lip turns (right)
*Project the board out of a
bottom turn as vertically up
the wave face as possible.
As the wave lip hits the
underside of the board,
lean back, sheet in, and
carve the turn with your
back foot. As the board
drops back down the face,
lean back a little to prevent
the board nosediving.*
Problems *This is not a
difficult move on small
waves. However, on big
waves great care must be
taken to make sure that the
breaking lip does not hit
the lee side of the sail. If it
does, an 'over the falls'
wipe-out will follow, and
could lead to extensive
equipment damage, or
even personal injury. To
avoid this try and time your
arrival at the critical section
a little earlier.*

Aerial off-the-lip turns
(left) *Using board speed
and the action of the lip
hitting the underside,
project the board into the
air, and turn it for re-entry
by weighting the front foot
and front hand.*

Backside off-the-lip turns
(below) *Carve the turn at
the wave lip by lifting with
your front foot and pushing
down with your back foot.
Lean into the sail and
toward the nose of the
board, ready for the drop
back into the wave.*

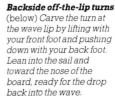

Bottom Turns

The bottom turn is executed at planing speed, at the base of a wave, and projects the board back up to the peak for a top or off-the-lip turn. The speed and positioning of the bottom turn determines how and where the board meets the lip or peak of the wave. It is very difficult to correct an inaccurate projection, and more often than not this will result in the rider having a nasty wipe-out. Bottom turns can be tricky in choppy conditions, and regularly result in spin-outs leading to the rider being 'sucked over the falls'.

If possible use a wave board that turns well, with a high aspect ratio, short boom rig. Ideal conditions are a Force 4-6, sideshore wind, with a quarter- to half-mast swell.

Bottom Turns

The frontside bottom turn Drop into the wave, and at the bottom carve the board away from the wind as if you were about to gybe. At this point the apparent wind (as determined by the speed of the board *and* the speed of the wave), combines with the true wind to put the board onto a broad reach – the fastest point of sailing.

Coming out of the turn you have two options. Either you carry on downwind in a straight line, across the wave face for a really fast ride, or you project back up to the peak for a top or off-the-lip turn. If the wave is peeling, you can turn back to the peak, but, if it is really critical it is probably safer to sail on 'down the line', and look for a less critical section. However, if the wave you have dropped into collapses along its entire length, or 'closes-out', do not attempt the bottom turn, but head straight for the shore until the water subsides.

Problems Sometimes in light wind conditions, board speed is lost coming out of the turn. This may be due to a change in wind direction, which means that as the board comes out of the turn, it is facing directly downwind.

The backside bottom turn When the wind is a cross onshore rather than a sideshore, it is very difficult to execute the bottom turn downwind, as the true wind will oppose the apparent wind created by the board and wave speed, leaving you seriously under-powered on the wave face. In these conditions it is better to reach across the wind, with your back to the wave.

To make a backside bottom turn, sail to the bottom of the wave and stall the board by shifting your weight back. At the same time carve hard with your back foot to project the board back up the face. This type of turn takes place at a much slower speed than the frontside turn, and is consequently much easier. Furthermore, it is used far more often due to the fact that perfect sideshore conditions seldom occur.

Craig Masonville (right top) *executing a severe bottom turn. He is leaning forward to maintain board speed. Note the amount of inside rail in the water. Robby Naish* (right middle) *about to spin-out. Only the very tip of the tail is touching the water. A narrower tail would have served him better. Maui Meyer* (right bottom) *making a bottom turn. Note the way his body is leaning into the wave face, with the sail clew just clear of the water. A backside bottom turn* (left) *by Robby Naish. The rig and body-weight are shifted back to stall the board, and redirect it up the wave face to hit the lip.*

Wave Jumping

Wave jumping is visually the most exciting aspect of the sport, and is not nearly as difficult as it might look. A satisfactory jump is within every windsurfer's reach – so go out and try one!

Jumping Technique

Wave jumping Sail at planing speed towards the wave, aiming for a section that is neither too critical or too flat. Plan your course so that the board hits the wave square on. Before you meet the wave unhook from your harness, and shift your weight onto your back foot, (both feet should be in their respective footstraps). As the board rises up the wave face shift your weight back further and lean your body toward the tail, sheeting out a little as you do. When the nose of the board clears the lip of the wave, pull up with your front foot and sheet out further. As the tail leaves the wave, relax the pull of your front foot and kick your back foot towards the wind. This will head the board off the wind and lower the tail slightly. While in the air constantly trim the sail, and keep the board off the wind by pulling up with your front foot and kicking out with your back foot.

To land, keep your weight back and the board off the wind so that you land tail first. If the landing is heavy, sheet out on touchdown and let yourself fall in, so that you can water start straight away.

In ideal conditions, (ie a Force 4-6 sideshore wind and a quarter- to half-mast swell), jumping is relatively easy. However, conditions are rarely ideal and there is always the chance that you will lose control at some stage of the jump. If this happens you should 'bail out', first making sure that your landing space is clear. To bail out, let go of the boom with both hands and simultaneously kick your feet out of the footstraps, pushing the board and rig away from you downwind.

Problems A common difficulty experienced when wave jumping, is that on take-off the board goes into a vicious nosedive. To prevent this, ease more power out of the sail just prior to take-off, and shift more weight onto your back foot. Sometimes the board 'spins-out' on landing. This is not the fault of the board's tail shape (as some people claim), but of the rider's technique! You *must* concentrate on kicking your back foot out into the wind, so that on landing the nose is downwind of the tail. This puts less pressure on the tail and therefore reduces the risk of a spin-out

In cross offshore wind conditions, the rig has a tendency to become over-powered going over the back of the wave. This is due to the extra wind created by the speed of the wave combining with the actual wind. Be sure to sheet out slightly while airborne, and watch out for gusts.

Peter Cabrinha (right top) demonstrating a flare jump, kicking the tail into the wind to prevent a spin-out on landing. Fred Haywood (right bottom) jumping in choppy conditions inside the surf line. His knees are flexed for extra control, and the windward rail is raised for added lift. Matt Schweitzer (left) jumping toward the shore at speed. Note how the windward rail is raised for extra lift. The wave is a 're-form' on the inside of the reef.

Jumping Technique

A unique view (above) from the boom end, of a flare jump. See how the back foot has kicked the tail out into the wind. A small jump (right top) on a re-formed wave inside the reef. Note the relaxed body position and the flexed knees.

Upside-Down Jumps

Although it looks impossibly difficult, the upside-down jump is within any competent wave jumper's reach. Given good conditions (eg a stiff Force 5 sideshore wind, and steep 2-4 ft (.6-1.2 m) wave faces), and a lot of determination it should not take long to master. If possible use a high aspect ratio sail and a board under 9½ ft (2.9 m).

The first time you make an upside-down jump will probably be by mistake, and the chances are you will have to bail out at the apex. However, this is in itself good practice, because the more you get used to bailing out the more you will be able to attack the jump with confidence. Remember, if in doubt – bail out!

Upside-Down Jumps

Approach the wave at planing speed, aiming for a steep section that you can jump before it collapses. As the nose of the board rises up the wave face, lean your body back and trim the sail. As the middle of the board leaves the wave lip, pull up hard with your front foot and lean your body right back.

As the tail leaves the wave, kick it up over your head and into the wind. When you reach the apex of the jump, and you and the board begin to drop, bring the tail back under your body, while keeping the sail sheeted in with you hanging underneath it. Aim to land the board tail first, keeping the nose off the wind.

Problems A mistake often made, is to mis-time the inverting of the board in the air. If left too late on the downward drop, landing becomes very difficult, and often results in a painful 'back flop'. The only solution is plenty of practice. If you are having difficulty in inverting the board at all, concentrate on finding the steepest part of the wave, and kicking your back foot overhead and into the wind.

Funboard Competitions

*Whether it is a high-speed slalom race in a
Force 7, or a man-to-man contest in mast high
surf, there is no sport more exciting to
participate in, or spectacular to watch, than high
performance windsurfing. It is the ultimate
challenge for the competitive sailor.*

Speed Trials

Speed trials As in many other sports, speed trials have consistently been responsible for major equipment and technique developments in the world of sailing. Traditionally frequented by hardcore enthusiasts, they have witnessed some of the strangest contraptions ever to float on water. The sailboard is a relative newcomer to this field, but has already left its mark.

Up until 1981, it was primarily the equipment that was on trial, but then the German high wind expert, Jurgen Honscheid, arrived on the scene. Turning up at the Weymouth Speed Trials with a surf-board he had picked up en route, he promptly broke the world record. Unfortunately his speed could not be recognized, as it was less than the 2% increase required, but it heralded a new era in sailboard speed sailing. The more bizarre craft disappeared, and the following year saw the record broken twice. By now it was apparent that the rider's technique was just as important as the equipment in determining the maximum speed reached. As the equipment used became more readily available, so speed trials moved within reach of more and more windsurfers. A comprehensive set of rules was drawn up by the Royal Yachting Association, which acts as the official authority for all world record attempts.

Fred Haywood The course consists of a 547 yd (500 m) run between two timing points. Ideally it should be set on a broad reach across flat water. The course that has produced the most records is that set at Portland Harbour, Weymouth, England, each October, to coincide with the equinoctial gales. In 1983, the record was 'smashed' here by the American, Fred Haywood, on a double spiral, concave hulled, board weighing less than 11 lb 4 oz (5 kg). Notwithstanding the strength and technique of Fred, and the skill of his board designer, Jimmy Lewis, the

year	venue	name	speed/knots	Km/hour
1977	Weymouth/UK	Derk Thijs	17.1	35.37
1979	Weymouth/UK	Clive Colenso	19.2	42.30
1980	Maui/Hawaii	Jaap van der Rest	24.41	45.16
1980	Veerse Meer/ Netherlands	Jaap van der Rest	24.45	45.50
1982	Brest/France	Philip Pudenz	26.55	49.13
1982	Weymouth/UK	Pascal Maka	27.82	51.52
1983	Weymouth/UK	Fred Haywood	30.82	57.12

Fred Haywood (above) blasting his way to 30.82 knots and the World Record at Weymouth in 1983. Pascal Maka (above left) making his attempt at Weymouth in 1983, and (left) 'The Record Breakers'. 'Gun running' across the bay (right).

Speed Sailing

big breakthrough was undoubtedly the introduction of the Wing mast. Other contestants had discovered that, using conventional rigs, it was just not possible to break the 27-28 knots barrier because they could not control the position of the sail draft accurately enough. The Wing surmounted this problem, and Fred got faster with every run.

No doubt there will be more Wings in evidence in the years to come, and, although most of the equipment used in this refined sphere is beyond most funboard sailors' means, they will benefit in the long run from the intense research and development speed trials encourage.

Speed sailing Riding a board at high speed is a sensation few ever forget. With your body leaning right out to counterbalance the rig, often only a short distance above the water, the sense of speed is phenomenal. The average wave board is capable of speeds of up to 25 knots in short bursts, and can really set the adrenalin going.

Transportation Making a speed run across a large bay requires the use of two cars. Take both cars to one end of the bay, leave one there, and drive back to the starting point. On completing the run, you can then drive back to the starting point again.

Equipment The ideal speed sailing board is a narrow tail, single fin, 'Gun', between 8-9 ft (2.4-2.7 m) in length. The tail width should be under 10 in (15 cm), and the widest point no more than 19 in (48 cm). It should have surf-board rails, with little or no rocker and an offset footstrap arrangement. Use it with a high aspect ratio, flat cut sail, a little on the large side to help the narrow board get moving.

Safety High-speed sailing can be dangerous, so never sail alone. Wear a wetsuit and carry some spare line, a replacement skeg (and screwdriver), and a spare universal joint in your harness backpack.

Wave Performance Contests

Of all the sailboard competitions, wave performance contests are the most visually spectacular. The bulk of the action takes place close to the shore, so the spectators can sense the element of danger and really judge how difficult some of the moves are.

The main drawback with this type of competition is, that due to media coverage commitments and the scheduling of other contests, it has strict time restrictions. This means that the organizers have to make do with whatever wind and wave conditions prevail, and these are seldom ideal. Potential competitors must realize this, and must be adequately prepared for any eventuality.

Contest structure The contest is structured on a simple man-against-man, knock-out ladder. The loser of each heat goes into a losers' bracket for a second chance, (a second loss means elimination from the contest). The winner of the winners' bracket competes against the winner of the losers' bracket to decide the overall result, but has to lose twice to come second. Each heat has four sailors on the water at the same time for 10 minutes, with the best two going through to the next round. The semi-final and the final run for 15-20 minutes.

Equipment Well prepared competitors have at least three boards at their disposal, a light wind floater, a strong wind sinker, and a big wave 'Gun'. They also have three rigs ready on the beach, with different sail sizes, so that an immediate change can be made in between heats. In addition they have a 'caddy', who is ready to sail a spare board and rig out to the competitor, should a breakdown occur during a heat. Well organized equipment preparation is the key to success in wave contests, and there can be no excuse for the often heard claim, 'there was not enough wind for my board'.

Always be ready and waiting for the starting signal of your heat. Most serious competitors wear a waterproof watch so that they can time their approach to the starting line exactly. Give your pre-heat approach a bit of thought, and try not to be caught way out to sea with 15 seconds to go, looking for a wave set.

Judging *Always try and find out what the judges are looking for; many have their own favourite moves. Watch other competitors (right top), and from their results try and determine what these moves are. If you lose a questionable judgment, (perhaps due to home town bias), never argue, and congratulate the winner – the sport is meant to be fun!*

Each pair of sailors is judged on transitions, jumps, and surfing, by three judges. Points are awarded for the degree of difficulty, the fluidity of execution and the flair of each move, out of a maximum of 10.

Transitions *Transitions consist of gybes, (including duck and one-handed), performed coming in on waves, and 'kick-out' gybes performed out of waves. A fluid duck gybe is considered more difficult than a conventional one, and consequently scores more points.*

Surfing (right middle) *Fluidity, control, and the ability to make critical moves determine the amount of points scored in the surfing section.*

Jumps (below) *Both level and upside-down jumps are permissible. Points are awarded for the height, carry, and complexity of the jump, and the control on landing.*

Starting (left bottom) *Two competitors setting off for the start of the O'Neill Wave Contest at Hookipa, Hawaii.*

World Cup and Euro Fun Cup

Funboard racing Funboard racing events, such as the World Funboard Cup and the Euro Funboard Cup, are usually divided into three self-contained sections that each account for a different percentage of the overall event – course racing (45%), slalom racing (30%), and wave riding contests (25%).

Unfortunately, in recent years these events have been plagued by extreme light wind conditions, and as yet have failed to produce the kind of exciting racing people would like to see.

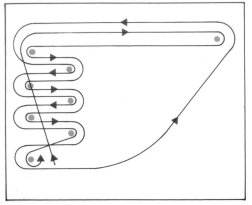

Course racing *The boards used in course racing are from the construction class, where there are no restrictions on equipment specifications. Hulls are often made from such exotic materials as Kevlar, carbon fiber, aluminum honeycombs, and pre-impregnated wood laminates. The lack of wind at many recent events has led to the 15 knots minimum wind requirement being reduced to 12 knots in some cases. This has brought about a new design approach, with many boards now having channeled hulls to promote early planing in lighter winds. Apart from the minimum wind speed requirement, the International Yacht Racing Union Rules apply.*

The course *For the Euro Funboard Cup (top), the course incorporates a short upwind leg, long, broad, and close reaches, and a downwind slalom leg. Each race takes less than 30 minutes to complete.*

Robby Naish (left middle) rounding a mark at Torquay, Australia, and (left bottom) a group of racers beginning the upwind leg.

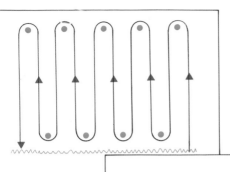

Slalom racing The slalom event usually requires a minimum wind speed of 20 knots, so that short sinkers or marginal boards can be used. A maximum of eight sailors compete in each heat, with the winner being decided on a knock-out basis. Each heat takes under 10 minutes to complete.

The course There are two types of the slalom 'ins and outs' course, one for flat water and one for surf. The short board surf slalom course (top) has marks set inside and outside the surf line. The competitors have to jump the waves going out, and ride or outrun them coming back in. Often with a Le Mans start, this is an excellent spectator event. An alternative course (top right) is a completely different shape, but is equally demanding in high winds.

Fraser Black and Richard Whyte (right middle) competing in a slalom race. Getting ready for a Le Mans start (right bottom) at Torquay, Australia.

Building a Funboard

Building a custom board is a highly specialized craft which takes years of dedication and practice to perfect. It would take a whole book to cover the subject comprehensively, so the following chapter simply outlines the basic steps involved, making use of readily available materials and standard DIY tools. With a little care and attention, a competent handyperson should be able to build a board that will handle well.

Shaping a board from a foam blank creates a great deal of dust, and many of the necessary materials are toxic and highly inflammable. For this reason, the most suitable location is a detached garage or large shed. Most of the materials used in the laminating process should be used at a room temperature of 68°F (20°C), so unless you live in a hot climate some sort of heating will be needed. However, this *must never* be a naked flame. Likewise, the use of these materials requires an efficient ventilation system, so choose your workshop accordingly.

Lighting is equally important. Fluorescent strip-lighting should be suspended overhead with the addition of some adjustable sidelights. By moving them around, these will help you to detect any unevenness on the top and bottom of the board while you are working on its shape. It is a good idea to have a cold water supply near at hand to rinse off any chemicals that might accidently get on your skin, or in your eyes. Protect the floor and work surfaces with PVC and keep a dry powder fire extinguisher at hand. Do *not* use a water extinguisher.

Tools It is possible to make a custom board with standard DIY tools which are easy to hire, borrow, or buy, if you do not already have them. In addition, for your own personal safety, you will need protective gloves, made either of rubber or disposable plastic. These should cover as much of your forearms as possible and should be used in conjunction with barrier cream. Eyes *must* be protected with safety goggles, and you will need a breathing mask to cover your mouth and nose. If you do get

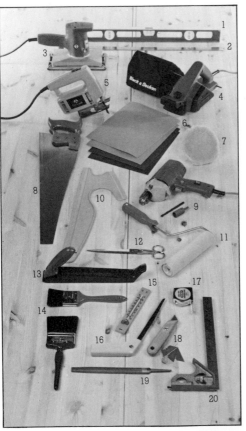

Tools *Building a custom board is not difficult, and can be accomplished quite easily with the following DIY tools: spirit level (1), flexible edge (2), electric sander (3), power plane (4), jigsaw (5), sandpaper (6), buffer (7), wood saw (8), electric drill and router (9), plastic squeegee (10), sponge roller (11), scissors (12), surform (13), paint brushes (14), thermometer (15), keyhole saw (16), tape measure (17), craft knife (18), file (19), set square (20).*

In addition, you will need a work-bench or trestles. These must be padded, to protect the board. When bonding the stringer into the blank, you can use roof-rack straps, or sash clamps.

Materials *Use the following: resin (1), milled fibers (2), masking tape (3), two pack polyurethane varnish (4), rubber gloves (5), face mask (6), syringe measure (7), mixing bucket and pots (8), coating* hardener (9), *non-slip coating (10), fiberglass cloth (11), hand barrier cream (12), acetone (13), safety goggles (14), coating resin (15), spray paint (16), the 'blank' (17).*

anything in your eyes, you must rinse it out immediately!

Materials To build a board first create its shape out of a plastic foam block, known as the 'blank'. You can either buy a commercially-made sailboard blank, roughly shaped with built-in rocker and stringers, or you can work on a block manufactured for the building industry as insulation. A professional shaper would use a sailboard blank as it is quicker and easier to shape, and comes in a variety of shapes and sizes. These are made from Polyurethane foam, and usually weigh about 8.8 lbs (4 kg) before they are laminated. The main advantage of the pre-formed blank, is that there is less excess foam to plane away, and it is a much more efficient medium for the professional shaper to work in. The main drawback is the cost, which may be as much as three times that of the insulation block. Assuming you opt for the latter, you have two choices, Polystyrene foam (PE), or rigid Polyurethane foam (PU).

Polystyrene foam is manufactured in two forms: expanded polystyrene, which has a small bead construction, and extruded polystyrene which is slightly more expensive. Both types are very fragile, and great care should be taken when using woodworking tools. Alternatively, polystyrene can be cut with a hot wire.

When laying up the fiberglass over the polystyrene, only use epoxy resin; polyester resin is *not* suitable. Epoxy resin has the advantage of having a slower hardening time, allowing you more time when laying up. It is stronger than polyester resin, but is more expensive and difficult to sand down after hardening.

Polyurethane foam is a rigid closed-cell foam, with a good resistance to water, which can only be cut with a saw and not a hot wire. However, it is very easy to work with. The outer skin of fiberglass laminate can be laid up with epoxy of polyester resin, but most professional board-builders use the latter. Great care must be taken to get the correct proportion of catalyst to resin when using polyester resin. The hardening time is much shorter than that of epoxy, so you will have to work faster. Finally, the top coat requires a special sanding coat to harden it.

Design

Design factors The reason for building a custom as opposed to a production board is to arrive at a board that exactly matches your particular requirements. What those requirements are is for you to decide They may depend on several factors. For instance, where do you normally sail? Is it on inland flat water, or do you like charging through the surf at the coast? How heavy are you? Can you water start? Do you want a floater or a sinker? Are you hoping to break the world speed record, or use the board to perfect your 'off-the-lip' maneuvers?

The earlier sections on board design and shapes will help you decide on the kind of shape you want to achieve. You may wish to make a lighter copy of a friend's production board, or copy someone else's custom board because the commercial price is too expensive for you. After all, the designers of these boards are highly experienced, only deciding on a shape after the exhaustive testing of several prototypes. Perhaps you are convinced of the value of some new, innovative, design that you have been considering for some time. Often people begin to think about building their own board once they have sailed a marginal 'pop-out' for a while, and now want to try out something a little smaller. If you are anxious about the feasibility of your design, use the design shown below, which works very well.

Designing the board First draw your design on graph paper showing the plan and side elevations, with cross-sectional elevation along various points of the board. Do this on small-scale graph paper on a scale of 1 to 10.

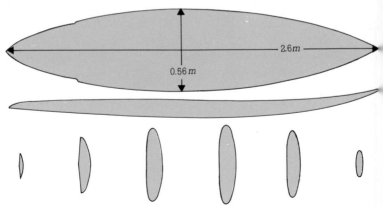

Now transfer the design to templates made of thick tracing-paper. Take your guide marks every ¾ in (2 cm) from your plan, dotting them every 8 in (20 cm) on the template. Join them up with a flexible rule, making sure all the curves run smoothly. Remember to take all measurements carefully from the center line. The plan view template should only be of one half, taken from the center line, to ensure symmetry.

The side-view template is used to mark out the profile of the stringer. Stringers are wooden spines made from ¼ in (6 mm) plywood or veneer, that are fixed in the foam blank to give the board rigidity. In this example a single stringer is used down the center line of the board, for simplicity, but you could use two either side of the center line, or even three with one down the center line, and one on either side. Remember that due to the camber on the top of the board, those stringers not on the center line will be shorter in height according to the profile of the camber.

Fitting the stringer Saw the foam blank in half lengthwise, taking care to keep the cut vertical. Having cut the stringer exactly to shape with a

Stringer and Blank

jigsaw or keyhole saw, sandwich it between the two halves of foam. Bond all three together with epoxy resin, making sure that the stringer does not protrude out of the blank at any point. Roof-rack straps can be used to clamp all three together while the resin hardens.

Depending on the depth of the blank, it is possible that the stringer may protrude above the top of the blank. The way to overcome this, apart from buying a thicker blank, is to bend up the front of the blank while the stringer is being bonded in. This can be done by holding down the middle and tail end of the blank with weights, and supporting the underside of the nose. When the resin has hardened and the straps have been removed, the rocker will be built in.

Shaping the blank Shaping the foam blank is not as difficult as you might at first imagine. Take your time and practice with the tools on scrap pieces of foam. Remember that although it is easy to remove areas on the board, it is almost impossible to put them back. In addition, bear in mind how fragile the foam is until it has the protection of lamination. Very often the foam has a hard uneven surface caused by the manufacturing process. This must first be removed and smoothed down with the plane. Constantly check with your spirit level for unevenness. Finally, sand down to the stringer with a long sanding block.

If the blank is thick enough, the scoop and rocker can be allowed for by positioning the stringer at an angle (left). Remember to leave at least a ⅜ in (1 cm) lip of foam all the way round the stringer, so that it does not overlap the blank at any point.

If you do not have any sash clamps, you can use roof-rack straps (right) to bond the two halves of the blank together. Be sure to put padding on the corners of the blank, or the straps will cut into the foam.

Template

Using the template Laying the blank underside up, draw in your center line down the middle of the stringer, and tape the half template of the plan elevation down its line. Rather than trying to draw round the edge of the tracing paper, it is easier to spray with aerosol paint round the edge so that the paint goes on the template and the outer waste foam that is to be cut away. Take care here, as many spray paints corrode the foam on contact. There are some available from art stores that are not harmful, it is however, a good idea to test a scrap piece of foam first. Spray from the direction of the center line outwards, holding down the edge of the tracing paper with a piece of scrap card. Then remove the template and repeat the process on the other side of the center line. Using the template in halves ensures symmetry. When the template is removed you will have a perfectly reproduced edge to work from, with no paint on the area of the blank to be retained.

Allowing for a little extra, cut out the shape of the board with the hand saw. Do not make the cut vertical but slant the saw blade out to the side at the bottom. This will make the deck slightly oversized, so as to allow for any miscalculations. Now plane down the side edges, working towards the correct line and check constantly with a set-square that the sides are at right angles to the hull. Then sand down the sides with a long sanding

Spraying around the template gives a more accurate outline than using a pen. Spray each side separately to ensure a symmetrical finish.

Making sure you leave a small margin, saw out the outline at an angle, so that the deck (on the bottom) is slightly oversized.

Plane the sides of the blank with a power plane, right up to the actual line of the spray paint.

It is very important that you constantly check, with a set-square, that the sides of the blank are at right angles to the top and bottom.

Side Profile

block at least 3 ft (91 cm) long. Using long strokes, you should be able to achieve a smooth flowing curve.

Mapping the side profile In order to mark out the side profile of the board on the walls of the blank, draw lines at right angles to the center line across the top of the blank at 2 in (5 cm) intervals. With a set-square take the lines down the walls of the blank. Now measure the depth of the stringer from the top of the blank at each point and transfer these measurements to the side line. If you do this for top and bottom you can then map out the side profile with a flexible rule.

Now shape the underside of the hull to sweep up at the front, and perhaps a little at the rear if you have some tail rocker. Use the plane working lengthwise down the board. Start from the center and work towards the edge lines, shaping one half at a time. Take your time, as it is very difficult to correct unevenness. Use your sidelights to check the sight line down the length and across the width of the board. Finally, sand down with a long sanding block, using 120 grain sandpaper, to a smooth curve. Apply the same procedure to shape the deck, planing from the center and sanding down. Use a length of sandpaper held between your hands to smooth out the rails. To finish, sand down the whole blank using 100 grain sandpaper until you have a satisfactory finish.

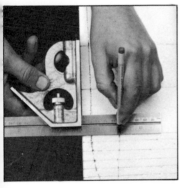

Map out the side profile of the board, by transferring the measured depth of the stringer in the center, to the side of the blank.

Working lengthwise, and away from the center, plane away the excess foam to form the scoop. The thicker the original blank, the more work this will entail.

Plane down the deck working outwards from the center, and blending the shape into the rail profile.

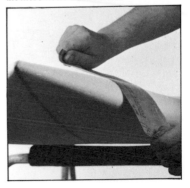

Carefully shape the rail profile by using a length of sandpaper held between each hand.

Decoration

Decorating the board After all the concentration involved in getting the shape right, now is the time to demonstrate your artistic flair. Painting a board can range from a few simple stripes to a visual masterpiece. The technique is to paint or draw on the blank so that the design shows through the resin coat when the board is laminated. Alternatively, a solid color can be achieved by adding pigment to the resin. Whatever you decide to do it is a good idea to use pale colors, as they are less likely to fade in the sun. Ultraviolet rays will turn the whole board yellow in time so try to use good quality resin, it is clearer than others. Again, be careful what spray paint you use on polystyrene as the thinner may eat into the foam. Always test your paint and fiber-tipped pens first on waste material. Several water-based and specialist paints are available in aerosol cans from art stores. These are often used for making models and are suitable for polystyrene.

You might like to paint your board with an airbrushing spray gun. Although these are quite expensive and take some time to master, they can produce the most amazing artwork on the board. Perfectly good results, however, can be achieved with can paint. Always take care to mask off all areas not intended for painting, as the spray dust gets everywhere. The simplest designs to produce are geometric, using different widths of masking tape and straight lines. This type of design can look very effective. An airbrush effect is also quite easy to achieve with aerosol cans spraying masked areas dark to light with one color, then blending them into another color by lightly spraying the new color from the light area into a new darker one.

Stencils Use stencils to decorate the board with shapes such as stars and circles. These can gradually become smaller towards the back of the board, or they can be random shapes. A shadow effect can be reproduced by moving the stencil slightly and spraying again in another or lighter color. Some shapers have their own logo screenprinted onto rice paper, which dissolves in the resin leaving only the color. They also sign and number the board at this stage.

Laminating The fragile, decorated, foam blank now has to be protected with its 'outer skin', the fiberglass lamination. Whether you are using epoxy or polyester the method is the same, except that you need to work faster with polyester as the hardening time is shorter. Using epoxy gives you more time but it requires much longer to harden, and needs very careful measuring of the resin to hardener mix. The masking tape

Stencils are a simple way of decorating the board, but you must mask off all other areas.

Offset the stencil on the second coat to give a shadow effect.

Laying Up

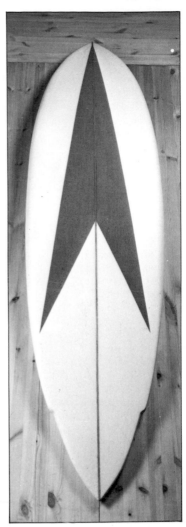

referred to in this section is not the type used in the painting section, but one used in fiberglass work. This does not dissolve when used with polyester resin.

Laying up the board The hull should be laid up first, which means masking off the deck with the tape and some plastic sheeting. Set the line of the tape back a little from the side rails on the deck, so that when you do the same on the other side you end up with two layers of cloth all the way round the rails. This gives the board extra strength in a vulnerable area. Place the board underside up, and lay the 6 oz (180 g) fiberglass cloth over the top so that it hangs down the sides. Trim off the excess cloth with scissors, as it is virtually impossible to cut later when soaked with resin. Smooth out the cloth with your hands, and trim it so that it just overlaps the masking tape line. Now do the same with the second piece of cloth, this time allowing a 2 in (5 cm) overlap. Cut 'V'-shaped nicks out of the cloth where there are any sharp corners. It is a good idea to reinforce the nose and tail with an extra 2 in (5 cm) square of cloth.

Resin

Before mixing the resin make sure all your tools are handy, and that you have applied the barrier cream to your hands and forearms. Wear the face-mask, and ask someone to help if necessary. Have the resin and hardener at a room temperature of 68°F (20°C), and mix up about 4½ lb (2 kg). Too much resin does not necessarily make the board stronger and it will definitely make it heavier.

Applying the resin Pour some of the mixed resin from a bucket along the center of the hull – not too much or it will just drip off onto the floor – and then work it outwards with a rubber squeegee. Take care not to pull up the cloth. Get your helper to work the resin into the cloth around the rails with a brush to save time. It should be saturated evenly so that no white or dry areas remain. Flatten out any bubbles that arise, and scrape off any surplus resin back into the bucket. Now wait for the resin to harden to a toffee-like consistency. The length of time depends on the air temperature and should be about one to two hours for polyester and two to three hours for epoxy.

While you are waiting, cut the excess resin away along the edge of the masking tape with a craft knife. Take care not to wait too long, as completely hard resin is extremely difficult to cut. After the cutting, polyester will take about two more hours to harden and epoxy four to five hours. When hard, file down and sand the rough edge. Only turn the board over when your are sure it is completely hard.

Lay the top of the board up in exactly the same manner as before using three layers on the deck, wrapping the cloth round the rails to give double thickness, and cutting it away along the tape. The only difference is that you need to reinforce the deck where you are going to stand with extra layers, especially in the foot strap area. Remember to clean all your tools with acetone before the resin starts to harden.

Exotic materials There are today, a number of hi-tech or exotic cloths available such as Kevlar or carbon fiber, which may be used instead of fiberglass, and are much stronger. Although they seem quite pliable, they are in fact much more difficult to work with, and are considerably more expensive. Kevlar (which is used in the manufacture of bullet-proof vests), is extremely difficult to cut, and tends to fray at the edges, especially after hardening, when it cannot be sanded down. It is therefore even more important to achieve a perfect fit before applying the resin. Although these materials have their uses for reinforcing areas, it is advisable to avoid them unless you are an experienced board builder.

Cut away the excess cloth while it is dry. Impregnated cloth is very difficult to cut.

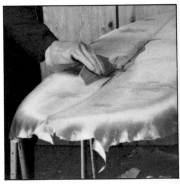

Use a rubber or plastic squeegee to spread the resin out quickly. Work it out to the edges.

Fin Boxes

Fitting the fin boxes With the help of the earlier section on fins you should by now have decided on the quantity and position of your fins. Taking measurements from your drawings, mark out the positions of the fin boxes on the tail of the hull. A single fin arrangement is used here, but the same procedure applies if there is more than one.

Cut through the laminated skin of the board with a craft knife and straight-edge, and then remove it leaving the foam blank exposed. Now cut a well out of the foam to accommodate the fin boxes you have purchased. This is best done with a router, or a grinder attachment on the electric drill. Cut the depth of the well deeper than the box, but make the width a good fit. Mask off round the sides of the well leaving a 5/32 in (4 mm) border. File this down at an angle of about 45°, and then fill it with resin. This will give the fin box lateral support. Then, check that the well is clean inside. Mix up a paste of resin and milled fibers and pour enough into the well to half fill it. Place two pieces of cloth, cut to the size of the well into the resin mix. Tape over the slit in the fin box and push it down into the well. The excess resin will squeeze up the sides of the box and run out of the top. Wipe this away *immediately*. Remove the tape from the slit in the fin box and carefully insert the fin. Check this with a set-square to make sure it is at right angles to the board. Tape up the fin from its tip to the rails of the board to hold it in position while the resin hardens.

Carefully check the positioning of the fin box, before cutting through the laminate with a sharp craft knife.

Fin boxes are available in different lengths. Make sure you use a good one.

When inserting the fin boxes, remove any excess resin immediately.

Taping up the inserted fin at right angles to the hull, will ensure that it is correctly set.

Finishing

Fitting the mast support You have a choice of two basic systems for holding the mast foot in the board. Either one or two deep, circular, cup-type wells which take the Mistral-type mast foot, or, another fin box, which takes the more popular nylon block-type mast foot. Here the latter system is used, following the same procedure as that for fitting the fin box underneath.

Finishing The next stage is to finish the surface of your board to protect it from the elements and, in particular, water. This is the most labour intensive part of the project, and will make or break the finished appearance of the board. After taping up the fin boxes, apply a coat of filler resin with a brush, and when it is dry sand it down by disc and then by hand. Then paint both sides with a coat of two pack polyurethane varnish, being sure to keep the surface free of fingerprints and grease. When dry, rub it down with wet-and-dry paper (working through from 400 to 600 grain), and soapy water, and buff it to a glossy finish with a lambs-wool pad. If you have done the job properly, you should have an immaculate professional finish. A non-slip area is needed on the deck where you are likely to stand. There are several ways to achieve this but the simplest is to mask off the outer gloss area first then apply a commercial non-slip clear paint.

Fitting the footstraps Once all the major work is finished, you can fit the footstraps. Again the number and position has to be decided. The best way to find this out is to sail the board. When you are sure of your foot positions make guide marks on the board. Straps can be attached in several ways. Some are glassed onto the deck, some are glassed into the deck, and others have special inserts that need to be set into the deck to retain the straps. The simplest method is to use one of the commercial types (preferably adjustable) that can be screwed into the deck. To do this, mark out where each plug should be set – your foot usually needs a width of about 5 in (13 cm) – then drill out the holes to the correct depth. Glue the plugs in with thickened resin and screw the straps into position.

Brush on the final coat of varnish, making sure that you cover the board evenly.

Sand down the whole board with a power sander, and then rub it down by hand using wet-and-dry paper.

The final look of the board depends on the amount of polishing and buffing-up. A good finish takes time to achieve.

Some professionals use sugar dissolved in resin for the non-slip deck, but the safest way is to use a well-known brand.

Protect the deck with tape, before drilling the holes for the footstrap plugs.

After filling the holes with resin, tap in the inserts for the footstraps.

There are a wide range of footstrap kits available. It is advisable to use the adjustable type.

Funboard Locations

Anywhere with plenty of wind and waves is a funboard location. From the exotic Hawaiian Islands to the sunny Mediterranean, from the busy Lake Garda in Italy, to the rugged Cornish coast in England, you will find keen windsurfers sailing their funboards, and testing their techniques to the full. New locations are being discovered every day, so why not go and find one for yourself!

Hawaiian Islands

The Hawaiian Islands *This island chain, located over 2,000 miles (3,219 km) west of California, is composed of five major islands. In summer, the Pacific High, a high pressure system with a clockwise rotation, produces easterly trade winds up to Force 6. From September to May large swells hit the north shores.*

Oahu Nine-tenths of the population live here. Kailua Bay is east-facing, and has good flat water for learners, and sometimes waves on the outer reefs. Usually only gets really windy in winter storms. The average wind in summer is Force 4.

Diamond Head, close to Waikiki, only works from March to October. Like all south-shore locations, it is affected by southerly swells in summer, and catches the east trade winds. If the wind is at all northerly, the surrounding cliffs make for gusty conditions. It is important to respect the regulars here; do not go out unless experienced.

Backyards, on the north shore at the point of Sunset Beach, is a very dangerous spot and not for beginners. A very nasty type of sea urchin breeds here, and a footful of its spines can make walking a misery for many months. The spot works on northerly swells and a northwest wind. The waves are very powerful, and the inside is shallow, so beware!

Maui Maui's twin mountains, joined by a flat plain give it a venturi wind effect. If the wind is Force 4 on Oahu, there is a good chance that it will be Force 5–6 on Maui, especially by midday, when the mountains have heated and the thermals have further increased the wind speed. In summer, Maui is very windy, but seldom has waves, except in unsailable parts of the south shore.

Near the airport are Kanaha and Spreckesville, the two best all round locations in the world. Both have flat water and an outside reef, which has waves between September and May. Hookipa, on the north shore, four miles (6.44 km) from the airport, is the most consistently challenging and windy spot regularly sailed. It is inadvisable for beginners to sail here. There are bad urchins, and a rocky headland where currents concentrate and boards are washed up after wipe-outs. Do come here on a good day, and watch the likes of Mike Waltze, Craig Masonville, Matt Schweitzer and other local stars make gravity-defying moves on the waves. The local surfers' rules are that they have right of way in any situation, and it is not permitted to sail if there are more than five surfers on one wave peak.

At Maalaea Bay, on the west side of the isthmus, there is only flat water sailing, but it is good for speed work. If the wind direction is northeast, then a Force 3 at Kanaha, after the afternoon thermals have accelerated it, will probably get up to at least Force 6 at Maalaea Bay. A boardsailing speed record, at 24 knots (44.47 kph), was set here in 1980.

Italy and France

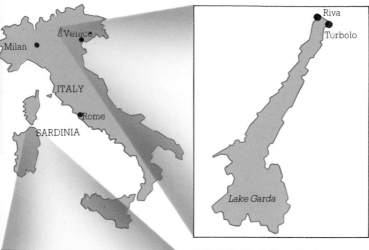

Italy: Lake Garda One of the few good funboard locations not on the sea, is this 40-mile (41.6km) long inland lake in the north of Italy, between Milan and Venice. It is surrounded on three sides by high mountains, producing excellent thermal winds. The Veneto blows from the north in the morning, and rarely gets above Force 3; then, after a period of calm around noon, the Ora blows up from the south, producing good winds of Force 4–8, with accompanying wave conditions. This pattern is fairly regular throughout the summer months.

Access is difficult in many places; the mountains rise steeply from the lake, and some hotels give access to residents only. The north of the lake, around Riva and Torbole, is generally regarded as the best location. Torbole has particularly good launching facilities.

There are many schools around the north of the lake hiring funboard equipment.

Italy: North-east Sardinia Offers some of the best funboard conditions in Europe. Porto Pollo has seen several international events. Isola dei Gabbiani has wave sailing and flat water. Both are best mid-May to June, September and October.

France Offers the choice of the consistent winds of the Atlantic coast, or the more powerful Mistral on the Mediterranean coast.

La Torche in south Brittany is highly rated for good wind and huge waves, especially in fall and winter. The long, sandy, exposed beach has good access from the sand dune car park, and spares, board hire and advice are available at Luc Mery's surf shop on the way to the beach.

Les Lecques and Port St Louis are good funboard spots on the Mediterranean coast. The first is a pretty village with good waves and even better cafés. Port St Louis is situated at the end of the Rhône Valley, where the Mistral gets a venturi effect as it is channeled down to meet the sea. This is a speed boardsailor's paradise.

Canary Islands and Japan

The Canary Islands This Spanish archipelago off the northwest coast of Africa can provide good funboard conditions most of the year, though spring and fall are best for a visit. The volcanic islands are served by the northeast trade winds, which can blow Force 4–7 daily, bringing a short swell during the spring and fall. In winter the trades can be augmented by the Sirocco, a hot wind from the Sahara. Though the air temperature is comfortable, the sea is never that warm, and you are advised to take a wetsuit.

Lanzarote
Lunar-landscaped island. La Santa, Playa de Famara, Playa Blanca and Playa de les Cucharas are good spots

Tenerife Best funboard spot is El Medano, with ocean swells and some flat water sailing. Playa de las Americas is famous for good surf breaks.

Fuerteventura Fuerteventura can offer a great deal to the demanding windsurfer. F2 have set up a test center, and many top sailors train here in winter. The north offers the best and most varied conditions; try Cotillo, Playas des Corralejo, and Isla de los Lobos.
Gran Canaria Playa des Ingles has good windy spots but no surf. For waves go to Maspalomas, and for peace, try Oro de Garza.

Japan Funboard sailing has become very popular in Japan recently. The small island of Nii-jima is its surfing capital, and worth the trip.
   Nii-jima is one of the southern chain of islands. It is reached by a four-hour boat ride from Tokyo. With its tropical black coral and black sand beaches, it offers some good summer swells and a consistent wind of Force 4 upwards. The island has played host to the Japan Cup event for the last two years.

UK and Australia

UK Devon and Cornwall have been recognized for years as having some of the best surf spots in Europe.

Devon Saunton Sands on the north coast has a three-mile (4.8 km) sandy beach, and excellent conditions. The gently shelving beach faces the prevailing southwesterly winds, and provides good surf and plenty of room to maneuver. Access is good, with parking lot.

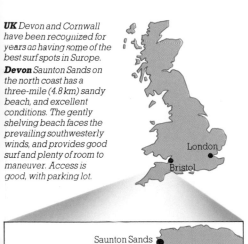

next to the beach, but prepare for a long walk at high tide.

The nearby small town of Braunton has long had surf shops and shapers, fast adapting to windsurfing. You will have no problem buying spares and renting boards. There are several custom board manufacturers.

Cornwall Many good wave sailing spots. Fall and spring are the most consistent seasons for waves and winds. Prevailing winds are southwesterly, but the coast is so varied that you can always find a bay with a crosshore wind not too far away.

Harlyn, being sheltered from the Atlantic, is a good spot for beginners to wave sailing. There are many good spots around Padstow. You can sail in the river mouth in most conditions, though a northerly at low tide is best. Newquay is well-known for its fine waves. Watch out for the surfers on home ground.

Australia: West Coast In December and January, hot convection currents from the desert create good afternoon sea breezes from the southwest. Cottesloe Beach, Perth, is good for windsurfing, but not waves. Along the coast, channels through the reefs give surf. Try Geraldton and Lanceton.

Torquay, Victoria A small town, south of Melbourne, Torquay hosts the annual 'Rip Curl and Quicksilver Wave Classic' each November. The most popular beach, Point Danger, offers relatively safe conditions, but the wind tends to be cross onshore.

Traveling with your board Part of the fun of windsurfing, is being able to sail in many different locations. If you are a keen and proficient sailor, you will undoubtedly want to take your own equipment with you. In the past, most airlines would carry your board and rig without causing too many problems, but as the sport has become even more popular, they have introduced some awkward restrictions. Many will now not carry a large board and mast, while others have imposed a 8 ft 4 in (2.5 m) limit on board length. Always check with the airline first before booking, and if possible, get acceptance in writing. You may find they charge for excess baggage, although the amount varies from airline to airline. If you are taking your board by air, make sure it is completely wrapped up and padded, and buy a strong board-bag with straps, so that it is easy to carry.

Technical Glossary

Apparent wind A 'wind' felt by the sailor when in motion. Its direction is determined by the speed of the board.

ABS Plastic material from which production boards are manufactured.

Aluminum Metal from which booms, masts, and universals are made. Ideal alloy for booms is 60/61 tensile.

Battens Removable fiberglass 'formers' to help the sail hold its shape.

Beating A point of sailing upwind, sailing as close to the wind as possible.

Blank Block of foam (either PU or PE), from which the board is shaped. When shaping is complete, the blank is laminated with fiberglass.

Carve Turning the board on the inside rail for a bottom turn, or gybe.

Cavitation Situation where air is drawn down the side of the skegs, causing them to lose grip, and the tail to slide away from the wind.

CE – (center of effort) The point at which the main force of the wind acts on the sail. When the CE is shifted forward, the board turns away from the wind: when it is shifted back, the board turns into the wind.

Clew The corner of the sail, located at the boom back end, to which the outhaul is attached.

Custom board A hand-laminated and hand-shaped board, produced individually to a sailor's specific requirements.

Downhaul Line attached to the tack of the sail, to put tension into the luff of the sail.

Draft Area of maximum camber in the sail. It influences the location of the CE.

Epoxy Resin used in board manufacture.

Eye of the wind The true direction from which the wind is coming. Tacking through this direction is called 'going through the eye of the wind'.

Extensions Aluminum pieces used to make masts and booms longer or shorter.

Fiberglass Material used, in conjunction with resin, to cover a foam blank in board manufacture.

Flare Either sinking the tail of a long board in a gybe, or kicking the back of the board into the wind in a jump.

Flat Term applied to a sail, the opposite of full. Flat sails are used in surf and strong wind conditions.

Flex Measurement of deflection in masts and skegs.

Floater A board that will support the weight of the average sailor when there is no wind, without sinking.

Foil The thickness in cross-section of a skeg or daggerboard. Maximum foil or thickness is usually at a point about one-third back from the leading edge.

Footstraps Loops of webbing, covered with neoprene, attached to the deck of the board to aid control while jumping and surfing.

Gybe Turning the board while going downwind, so that the tail of the board passes through the eye of the wind.

HAR – (high aspect ratio) Name for tall, short-boomed sails.

Harness Accessory designed to take the strain off the sailor's arms. It is strapped to the body, with a hook on the chest, which is hooked into a loop on the boom.

Head Top third of the sail. The shape of the head is critical, and should be flat to aid control.

Hull The board, excluding the rig and daggerboard.

Inhaul Line attaching the boom to the mast.

Kevlar An ICI fiber, derived from a type of nylon, which is stronger than fiberglass. It is used in conjunction with resin in board manufacture.

Knots – (nautical miles per hour) A nautical mile is 6,080ft (1,853m), as opposed to 5,280ft (1,609m) for a statute mile.

Lamination The joining of layers of one substance to another. In board manufacture the word applies to the lamination of fiberglass to the blank, and in sail manufacture it applies to the lamination of Dacron to Mylar.

Leech The area of the sail that runs from the clew to the head, usually supported by battens.

Luff The area of the sail that runs parallel to the mast.

Luff perpendicular The distance from the clew to the boom attachment point.

Mast foot Part that attaches the power joint to the board.

Nose The front of the board. In nautical terms – the bow.

Outhaul Line attached to the clew grommet and boom back end, and used to flatten or trim the sail.

Plane Sailing over the surface of the water, with minimal displacement at high speed.

Polyethelene A thermoplastic used in board manufacture. May be

'roto-molded' or 'blow-molded'.

Pop-out A production fiberglass board, made in a two-piece or three-piece mould.

Power joint A rubber joint attached at one end to the mast base, and at the other to the mast foot.

Rails The sides of the board.

Reaching A point of sailing across the wind.

Resin Substance used to impregnate fiberglass or similar materials, to give strength and rigidity.

Rig The mast, boom, and sail.

Roach The area of the leech beyond the perpendicular from the clew to the head, supported by battens.

Rocker The amount of upwards curve in the nose and tail. It influences the turning and wave-handling abilities of the board.

Set The fine turning of the rig, which determines the shape of the sail.

Shaper A person who shapes blanks, and designs prototype boards.

Sinker A board that will not support the rider's weight when there is no wind, and in fact will sink.

Skeg A fin or fins at the tail of the board. Its function is to aid directional stability, and prevent the tail from sliding away from the wind when pressure is applied by the back foot.

Spin-out The same as cavitation.

Tacking Turning the nose of the board through the eye of the wind, while beating to reach a point upwind.

Tail The rear part of the board. In nautical terms – the stern.

Universal joint A combination of the mast foot, power joint, and mast base.

Wave Sailing Glossary

Aerial To leave wave face, and come back down on same face; a difficult move.

Animal Wave sailor whose sole objective is to destroy wave faces.

Backside To sail across wave face with back to wave.

Bailing out Abandoning board, to avoid injury, while airborne or on critical part of wave.

Beachbreak Waves breaking directly onto beach, creating hazardous rips. Difficult to negotiate on sailboard.

Bitchin' Expression used to describe high quality conditions.

Bottom turn Fast, carved, turn at base of wave.

Bowling Description of a section of a wave that breaks or closes-out in a bowl shape. Difficult to negotiate.

Caught inside Being unable to make it outside the breakline, when a large set comes in.

Close-out Collapse of long section or whole wave.

Coral Sharp and unforgiving animal on which waves break.

Crosshores Wind blowing perpendicular to the waves, ideal conditions for surf sailing.

Cutback Fast transition, where board is turned at top of wave to go back down face.

Drilled Getting caught by a wave and often being pushed to the bottom.

Eating it Same as getting drilled.

Frontside To ride the wave, facing the wave's face.

Geek Sailor who lacks competence, and gets in everyone's way, or is simply big-headed.

Getting air Same as aerial, applied to wave jumping.

Gnarly Expression used to describe dangerous or difficult conditions.

Gun Board with drawn-out outline for big waves.

Inconsistent Variable conditions, for example a Force 6 one moment, and a complete lull the next.

Kick out To leave wave after a move or series of moves, before it collapses, to avoid getting caught inside.

Kill it! Command given to competent wave sailor to destroy wave faces.

Kook As in geek – possibly worse.

Lacerating Description of a series of carving transitions on wave face, throwing up large quantities of water.

Late drop Catching a wave just before it breaks, and only just reaching the bottom in time.

Lifeguards They police the beaches and save lives – heed their advice!

Lip bash Hitting the lip late and hard while surfing a wave.

Locals Have respect for them – they were there first!

Mushy A wave that breaks prematurely because of onshore wind.

Off-the-lip A cutback at the lip of the wave, usually results in large quantities of water being thrown into the air.

Offshores Offshore wind, creating good surfing conditions, but very difficult and dangerous surf sailing conditions.

'Over the falls' Being sucked up the wave face, and pitched out by lip. Will result in being drilled, dragged, pounded, or all three.

Peak The point at which the wave begins to break.

Peaky Waves breaking everywhere.

Peeling Description of a wave that breaks constantly from one end to another. Best for wave sailing or surfing.

Pitched Being bodily thrown out with lip of wave – (see 'over the falls').

Pitching Condition where the lip of the wave throws out and lands in front of the wave face, thus forming a tube.

Pounded Getting thrashed by the wave, often off the bottom. Very unpleasant, regular occurrence in beachbreak conditions.

Radical Expression used to describe attempt at difficult move, or to describe dangerous conditions.

Reef rash Grazes or lacerations caused by being dragged across a reef.

Reefbreak Waves breaking on a rock or coral reef. There is usually an area of relatively calm water between the beach and the reef.

Rip Current caused by waves or tide. Visible as short, steep, chop.

Ripping Making a series of spectacular moves, strung together on one wave face, often throwing up large quantities of water.

Sharks Creatures which eat fish – but if one is around, do not take risks!

Shorebreak Waves breaking on beach.

Shoulder (of wave) The end part of a wave which has not yet broken.

Shredding (see lacerating).

Sideshores (see crosshores).

Slashing (see ripping).

Stoked Having a feeling of euphoria after a session in premium conditions.

Sucking up A hollow wave breaking on reef or beach, very dangerous. (See 'over the falls'.)

Surf rat Fanatical addict who lives only for sufing or wave sailing.

Tearing (see ripping, slashing).

Thruster Tri fin arrangement on surf or sailboard.

Toad To take off and die, dropping in too late into a wave. (See 'over the falls'.)

Tube Created by the lip of the wave pitching out and landing in front of the base. Possible to negotiate on a surf-board, impossible on a sailboard.

Urchins Creatures with sharp poisonous spines. Do not step on them!

Vertical Vertical moves on wave face. (See ripping, slashing, and tearing.)

Warning signs Heed them!